72 HOURS TO THE JOB YOU LOVE

Secrets to Landing your Dream Job

MyJobMag

MyJobMag

Just like most books that you have read, you don't bother to read the dedication page because once again the book is dedicated to someone you don't even know. Well, this is different. Because you are the reason we decided to write this book in the first place. This book is dedicated to the hundreds of thousands of job seekers who are yet to get an opportunity to contribute to the success of an organization. To millions of job seekers whose job search efforts has for some reasons not been able to see the light of the day.
This one is for you.

INTRODUCTION

Landing a job in a competitive market can be quite challenging, but at the same time, a lot of job seekers underestimate the time and energy that has to be invested into finding a job. Tackling the challenge of landing a job can be well within your grip if you put in the work to follow job search tips and guidelines.

This book is broken down into sections providing you with resources that will help you enter into the world of work with assurance. The different sections of this book are chronologically arranged into different steps that needs to be taken in the job search process that will enable you to finally land the job of your dreams.

Every section of this book is packed with hints, tips and assessments to make sure you are fully equipped and prepared to enter into the world of work and finally land the job of your dreams. There are useful examples and templates that will guide you at every stage of your job search journey.

This book begins by analyzing ways to start your job search journey. It is not enough to hurry into searching for job vacancies online when you don't even know what you want to do and also not in any way prepared for the task that is to come when you eventually get the job. Once you have been able to examine yourself and discover the kind of job you want to do, then the process of working to make your dream job a reality becomes easier.

Once you are able to discover your career objective (i.e. you have discovered the kind of job you would love to do, where you would likely love to work, and the kind of environment that works best for you), your job search will have a direction.

As soon as you discover what you want to do, learning how to find available jobs should be the next step for you. It is not enough to depend on job advertisement alone as 80% of available jobs are not advertised. While you search for job vacancies online, open yourself up to creating connections and building networks with people.

Once you have been able to identify a job that you want to apply for, an application must be sent attaching your CV and cover letter. A guide on how a CV and a cover letter are written is included in this book. Note that every single application must be tailored to the job that you are applying for.

This book progresses to equip you with tips and steps to help you prepare for an interview. This includes tips about carrying out employer research to preparing for commonly asked job interview questions and the practice of getting ready for a job interview.

Finally, tips on how to create a great first impression on your new job as well as how to succeed in the first 90 days of your new job are well-covered in this book.
Also, all the sections of this book include assessments to ensure you have a good grasp of any topic discussed. Following all the sections of this book diligently in chronological order will definitely increase your chances of getting a job.

CONTENTS

CHAPTER 1

SELF EXAMINATION

No doubt, starting a job search journey can be tiring and over-whelming, that is why it is important to start with the most important aspect of the journey...which is you!

Self-examination has to do with knowing and understanding your personality, professional values, interests, skills and achievements.

It is almost impossible for you to engage in a successful job search without knowing who you are. If you don't know who you are, then who are you going to tell the employer about? You need to have a great understanding of who you are to be able to articulate the same knowledge to your prospective employer. Starting your career journey, it is good for you to do a good self-assessment to discover yourself. Assessing yourself is not a difficult thing to do. You can start by asking yourself some basic questions like:

·   What drives me?
·   What do I like doing?
·   What is important to me?
·   What can I do well?
·   What do I look forward to achieving?
·   What roles am I most suited for?
·   What kind of life would I love to live?

Are you trying to answer these questions already? It is okay if you don't have the answers to the questions right now. Just make sure you take note of the questions as you go through the assessment tests in this chapter.

These assessments are designed to help you examine yourself, which is the most important step in engaging in a successful career journey.

What would you like to do?

If you want to properly examine yourself, then it is time for you to take a moment and reflect on your answers to these questions. You can use the space in the table on the next page to quickly jot down all that you would like to do from as far back as you can remember, till now.

You may run out of space trying to write down all that you would love to be, just remember to make use of the space wisely to put down your most important or recurring career path. Do you know why? It is simple; if you look closely at all what you have written, you will notice that some attributes are common amongst all the careers that you have written down. Even if your list is that long, list the most important ones and keep the rest in mind as you go on in this chapter.

WHAT DO YOU LIKE TO DO

1.

2.

3.

4.

Figure 1.0 *Self-examination assessment, make a simple list of the things you would like to do.*

1.1 UNDERSTANDING YOUR VALUES

Values are the foundational strongly-held beliefs and ideas that people consider important. Different people have different values. Values shape the way people view the world and what they consider good or bad.

Sometimes people maintain their values throughout their lifetime while others may change their values or find some of them less important.

Values are very important, but most times, we are not even aware of them and we, therefore, take them for granted especially during our job search journey. Finding a career that fits with your values has a lot to do with how satisfied you will be on the job eventually. Accepting a job that does not match with your values may put you in a disadvantaged position in the future.

Values are formed early in life and can be shaped by our family, friends, culture, education, religion etc. When you are taking the following assessment, be sure to fill in your most important values.

Since we are concentrating on the job search process, it is good that we focus on not just your values but your workplace values. The question here is how can you determine your workplace values? This assessment will help you determine your workplace values in simple steps.

Workplace Values Exercise

This exercise is a 3-step process that is designed to help you discover your workplace values. Feel free to put down the correct information as no one is watching or going to score you.
Let's get right into the exercise:

Step 1

Below is a list of workplace values. You would have to rate or place your importance on these workplace values using the scale below.

1 = Very essential
2 = Essential to me
3 = Not really essential to me
4 = Not essential to me

Workplace Values	Scale 1-4
Solve problems and help others.	
Continuously learn and improve on myself.	
Be innovative/ come with ideas and create new things.	
Constantly challenge myself mentally.	
Balance my work/career and my family life.	
Express my physical rather than mental strength.	
Reward hard work, dedication, and excellence.	
Ensure work stability and security.	
A fair compensation structure.	
Ensure that my efforts are recognized and fairly rewarded.	
Have a great impact on other people, most especially the society.	
Apply my creativity, imagination and innovation to my day - to - day tasks.	
Ensure a friendly and warm working environment.	
Emphasize the importance of team work.	
Allow me work with deadlines and some amount of pressure.	
Ensures a peaceful environment, where I can work with comfort and peace.	
Allow me interface with people in the course of my day – to- day tasks.	
Afford me the opportunity to use technological tools and techniques that are relevant to the work that I do.	
Afford me the opportunity for leadership and mentoring.	
Give me the opportunity to make decisions in the course of performing my task.	
That places emphasis on respecting individual personalities.	
That will give room for adventure, fun and excitement.	
That will give me the opportunity to grow and a tolerance for error during my growth process.	

Figure 1.1.0 *Understanding your values. This table consists of a list of workplace values to guide you in discovering yours.*

We understand that this is a long list of values. We decided to create this long list to make the process even easier for you, so you don't have to think too much about what workplace values you should write down. Let's move to the next step of this assessment.

Step 2

Since we have already created a list of workplace values, all you will have to do here is simple. From the values that we have listed above, you would have to pick 10 values that are most important to you and mark them. (You can use a circle to mark them).

This is easy to do right? Then, let's move to the next step. Write these workplace values in the space below.

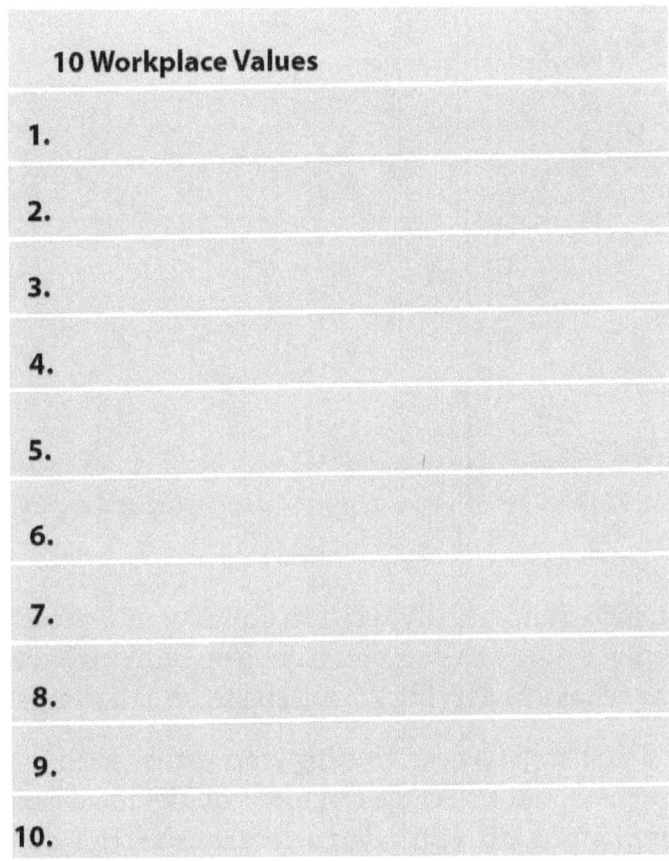

10 Workplace Values
1.
2.
3.
4.
5.
6.
7.
8.
9.
10.

Figure 1.1.1 *Workplace values discovery. Fill the table with your workplace values from figure 1.1.0 above.*

Step 3

Now that you have listed your 10 most important workplace values, then it's time for you to narrow down these values. At this stage, you have to re-visit your list of the 10 most important workplace values and reduce it to 5. How do you do this? It is simple; you need to look at your list and then select 5 most important workplace values from the 10 that you have already created earlier in the space that follows.

5 Workplace Values
1.
2.
3.
4.
5.

Figure 1.1.2 *Workplace discovery assessment. Make a list of 5 workplace values from figure 1.1.1*

Once you have successfully written down your 5 most important workplace values, then you have been able to successfully determine what a satisfying job will be to you to a large extent.

This is the first step to determining your career path in your job search journey. You know that before you decide a career path or even apply for a job, you have to determine if the job will be a good fit for you right? This is what you will be able to achieve at the end of this chapter.

What did you discover?

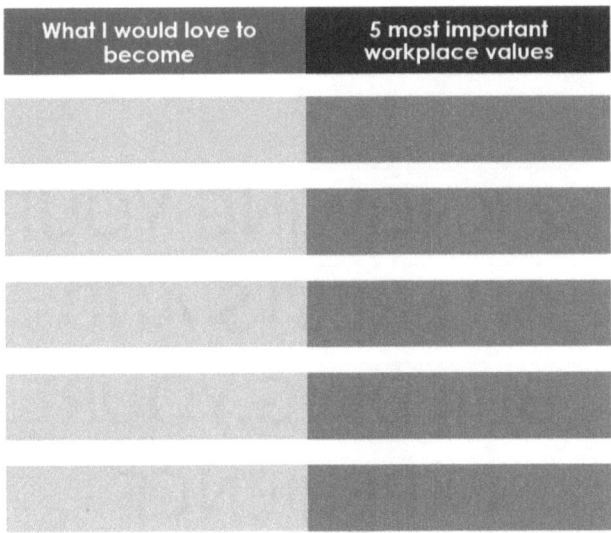

What I would love to become	5 most important workplace values

Figure 1.1.3 *Career choice assessment. This table includes details from figure 1.0 and figure 1.1.2, it is a simple comparison of the two tables.*

Did you notice that they were quite conflicting? If so, you will find out why as you go through the remaining aspects and exercises in this chapter.

1.2 KNOWING YOUR INTERESTS AND BUILDING YOUR EXPERIENCE

Knowing your interests

Everyone is interested in one thing or the other regardless of what it is. I know that some things interest you more than others. You know why? It is because you are different.

Interest is a feeling that causes you to focus or pay attention on certain objects, events, people or processes more than others.

Are you wondering why we are talking about interest in this chapter? Well, it is simply because discovering what intrigues you will further help you examine yourself to know the kind of jobs that you would naturally be drawn to. If you critically look at yourself, you would notice that you have made use of your interest several times maybe without even noticing it. Deciding on where you would love to hang out, the music to listen to etc. When you are doing something that you enjoy, it is easier for you to pay attention and feel motivated because your interest is the drive. This also applies to your career.

To help you identify your interest as it relates to you career, you will have to take a few assessments to help you with your career decisions. First of all, we would love you to make a list of things that you are interested in below:

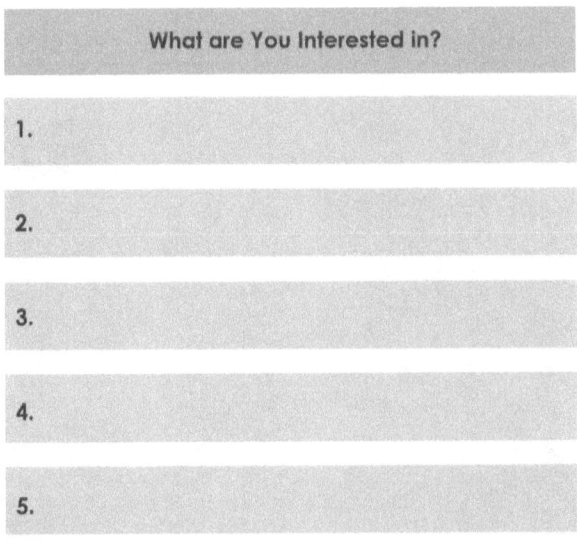

Figure 1.2.0 *Knowing your career interests. Write down the things that interests you in the table above.*

To help you create a list or ideas of what your interest may be, we have created a list that you can make do with on the go. You can use the scale below to determine your interest from the interest list below:

4 – Strongly agree
3 – Agree
2 – Neutral
1 – Disagree

Interest	Scale 1-4
I love solving problems.	
I love teaching People.	
I am Passionate about learning.	
I am keen about innovation.	
I have a great passion for numbers.	
I love helping people.	
I enjoy leading others.	
I enjoy making decisions.	
I love public speaking.	
I enjoy connecting with people.	
I love writing a lot.	
I love to be creative about the things that I do.	
I really enjoy working outdoors.	
I am very passionate about nature.	
I love to keep a clean and tidy environment.	
I love travelling a lot.	

Figures 1.2.1 *Examining your interest. This table consist of a list of interest that will guide you in discovering yours.*

Building your experience

At the mention of 'work experience', an average job seeker is scared. Well, we understand that sometimes employers make work experience look like an insurmountable mountain. Regardless of how gaining a work experience has been presented to you, we cannot still argue against the fact that building your work experience is an essential aspect of landing a job.

Forget about the name "work experience". An experience is an event or occurrence that leaves an impact or lasting impression on you. For example; if you have spent a long time with your mother making cakes, after a while, you would notice that the event of cake making would have rubbed off on you. This simply means that you have an experience in cake making, that is it. This is what an experience is all about. So if you transfer this same approach to your career, you would realize that you are already talking about your work experience.

It is that simple!

The difference is that the knowledge that you are transferring here is related to the career path that you will decide to follow. Activities that you have engaged in or carried out in the past is what will add up or form your work experience.

So you would take an assessment that will help you reflect on some activities that you have engaged in.

Activities	Date Range/Educatonal Level	Knowledge Gained/Skills Acquired	Likes	Dislikes
E.g. Heading the press Club Project.	Secondary School	Learned practical leadership and organizational skills.	Enjoyed the opportunity to lead people towards achieving a goal.	None, I enjoyed the entire process.

Figure 1.2.2 *Building your experience. Use the guide in the table above to discover your work experience.*

Step 1

The table above will guide you on reflecting and writing down activities that you have engaged in:

Note: Feel free to add your volunteering, internship and even paid job experiences to the list above.

Step 2

After you must have finished filling the sheet above, the next thing for to do is to create a list of your likes and dislikes. Creating a list of your likes and dislikes means forming a 'likes' and 'dislikes' list from the sheet you filled earlier.

You will have to fill in your top 5 likes and dislikes below.

Likes	Dislikes

Figure 1.2.3 *Knowing your likes and dislikes. Put down your likes and dislikes in the table above.*

1.3 DISCOVERING YOUR SKILLS

Most likely, you must have heard about skills; if so, what is a skill? Well, a skill is an ability and capacity needed to intentionally and systematically perform a task or carry-out an activity. Skills are things that you do or learn how to do that helps you do other things. Do you know that you can pick up skills from different places? Yes, you can.

You can pick up skills through work experience, study or simple activities that you do in your spare time, etc. Many times, you must have picked up different skills without even recognizing it. Your ability to recognize your skills will make it easy for you to know the kind of job that you would love to do.

You may have lots of useful skills, but maybe they don't just come from jobs. Discovering your skills will go a long way to help you discover the job that is right for you. For this reason, we will walk you through some assessments that will help you discover some amazing skills you never imagined you have.

Before we go into the assessment, it is good we establish that skills are broadly divided into two-: hard skills and soft skills (transferable skills). So what are hard skills and soft skills?

Hard Skills

You must have heard about hard skills and maybe you have wondered what they are. Just as the name implies, hard skills are teachable skills set and abilities that are measurable. Hard skills are simply the technical abilities that fit a job. Hard skills can be acquired through formal teaching (classroom teaching), online courses, educational materials, and even on the job.

For example; hard skills needed for an accounting job will include asset management, accounting analysis, etc.

Soft Skills

On the other hand, soft skills are skills that are not so tangible. These skills are not required to do any particular job. Soft skills can be acquired through various means like; environment, work experience education, etc.

Soft skills are also referred to as interpersonal skills. Unlike hard skills, soft skills are not easy to measure and evaluate. Soft skills include communication skills, listening skills, empathy, etc.

Since we have understood that skills are divided into two, it is time for us to get right into the assessment.

Assessment

Step 1

Now, using the table below you would have to rate your current competency in each skill listed below on a scale from 1 to 5. You would have to identify the skills you would need to develop.

Figure 1.3.0 *Discovering your skills. Fill the table above to discover your skills.*

Organizational Skills	Self Rating (1 - 5)	Indicate whether or not you would love to acquire any skills (Indicating with yes or "no")
I love organizing people, events, and things.		
I enjoy classifying information.		
I love sorting information.		
I am good at co-coordinating resources.		
I enjoy streamlining procedures.		
I like researching and gathering information.		
Total	----30 -----%	

Leadership Skills	Self Rating (1 - 5)	Indicate whether or not you would love to acquire any skills (Indicating with yes or "no")
I love leading groups.		
I am great at building teams.		
I don't mind bearing risk on behalf of everyone.		
I enjoy delegating power to empower other people.		
I am keen on innovation.		
I enjoy inspiring others.		
Total	----30 -----%	

Figure 1.3.1 *Discovering your skills. Fill the table above to discover your skills.*

Problem – Solving Skills	Self Rating (1 - 5)	Indicate whether or not you would love to acquire any skills (Indicating with yes or "no")
I enjoy analyzing problems.		
I take time to understand the cause & origin of a problem.		
I like to try out new ideas and things.		
I love to research about things a lot.		
I feel satisfied creating solutions.		
Total	----25 -----%	

Figure 1.3.2 *Discovering your skills. Fill the table above to discover your skills.*

Technical Skills	Self Rating (1 - 5)	Indicate whether or not you would love to acquire any skills (Indicating with yes or "no")
I enjoy working with numbers.		
I have a great passion for data analysis.		
I am good with computer operations.		
I enjoy providing technical support to people around me.		
I enjoy building things.		
Total	----25 -----%	

Figure 1.3.3 *Discovering your skills. Fill the table above to discover your skills.*

Interpersonal Skills	Self Rating (1 - 5)	Indicate whether or not you would love to acquire any skills (Indicating with yes or "no")
I create relationships with people easily,		
I love to make everyone around me active and agile.		
I don't like to see people around me struggle, so I always help.		
I am good at influencing others.		
I always love to respond to other people's ideas.		
Total	----30 -----%	

Figure 1.3.4 *Discovering your skills. Fill the table above to discover your skills.*

Creative Skills	Self Rating (1 - 5)	Indicate whether or not you would love to acquire any skills (Indicating with yes or "no")
I am usually enthusiastic about learning something		
I enjoy using my imagination a lot.		
I enjoy finding a new way to solve a problem.		
I love to communicate my ideas through writing.		
I take time to reflect on ideas.		
I really don't like to follow rules.		
I believe that everything exists in my mind.		
I am usually inquisitive; I believe that there is a reason behind everything.		
I enjoy building learning material		
I am passionate about drawing and painting.		
I enjoy music a lot.		
I am passionate about graphic design.		
I always love to challenge stereotypes.		
I always look forward to trying new things.		
Total	----70 ----%	

Figure 1.3.5 *Discovering your skills. Fill the table above to discover your skills.*

Step 2

Now that you have filled the tables above and calculated the calls for all categories, now it is time for you to examine your top skills.

Looking at the table above, write your top 5 skills below.

If you have written down your top 5 skills, you can make it even more tangible by taking a simple exercise. This exercise will simply guide you on how you can relate your top skills to tangible real-life situations.

For example; *"I organized an awareness event for all job seekers during my service year and invited HR Managers to educate us on the world of work. I figured that there were some things we did not understand about job search and the event would be of help to every one of us"*.

If you look at the example above, you would notice that the candidate has successfully created a concrete and tangible situation. So, what next? The skills demonstrated through this example include problem-solving, interpersonal, leadership and communication skills.

1.4 FINDING OUT YOUR ACHIEVEMENTS

Can you remember one thing you have done that you are proud to put your name on?

Achievements are things that you accomplish especially by putting in great effort or through a special skill or qualification. Achievements simply have to do with things that you have done that have a lasting impact on you, other people, or other things.

Achievements show that you have taken an initiative to perform a task or do something in the past that can also influence your future successes. Discovering your achievements is also a step forward to understanding yourself and the job you would love to do.

Now, you will take some assessments to help you discover your achievements and how you can properly communicate them to your prospective employer. If you can't remember achieving anything, then the following questions can help you recall some of the achievements that you may not even be aware of.

· Can you remember receiving an award, title, trophy, etc. as a form of recognition for something that you have done?

· Have you ever come up with a solution to a problem that would have caused damage if you had not intervened?

· Have you ever made any suggestion that resulted in a positive change?

· Have you ever innovated something?

· Have you ever taught someone something?

Once you have been able to identify some of your achievements with these questions, then you can use the S.T.A.R method to write them out briefly and clearly.

S –Situation (Give a brief overview of the situation).
T – Task (Outline the specific task and the responsibility you were faced with).
A – Action (Systematically explain the actions you took and why you took them).
R – Result (Outline the result of the actions that you took in clear terms using figures, percentages, etc.).

An example of an achievement using the S.T.A.R method is given below, so that you can have a better grasp on how you can also form and put down your achievements.

Situation
The supermarket where I worked previously did not focus on communicating new products to their customers, as it was no one's duty.

Task
I talked to my supervisor about it and she permitted me to do what I feel is good. So, I decided to look for ways to communicate new products to our customers.

Action
When new suppliers bring in new products, I take my time to sort them and place their banners at the front of the supermarket and their fliers on the reception table. I also made use of the new product tag to identify them as new products.

Result
The supermarket had a 10% increase in sales because some customers decided to try out some new products from seeing the adverts. The supermarket was also able to sell new products faster than they would normally.

Use the S.T.A.R method to fill three of your achievements in the table below:

Figure 1.4.0 *Finding out your achievements. Fill the table above to discover your career achievements.*

1.5 UNDERSTANDING THE KIND OF WORK ENVIRONMENT THAT YOU CAN THRIVE IN

We understand that this chapter is all about you, but you should also realize that you are eventually going to be working in a place with different people.

A job is not just about what you do. The people you work with and the environment you work in can determine your success or failure to a large extent. That is why it is good for you to understand the kind of environment that will fit your personality and bring out the best in you.

The assessment below will help you understand the kind of people you will enjoy working with. Ready? Let's start!

Work Environment Assessment

Imagine you walk into a gathering of people sitting in different groups, and you are the only new person that doesn't have a group yet. If you have to join a group, looking at the different groups' categories below which group will you likely join?

The table below will give you the information you need to know about the different groups of people. Read the characteristics of the different groups carefully and choose the one you would most likely be drawn to?

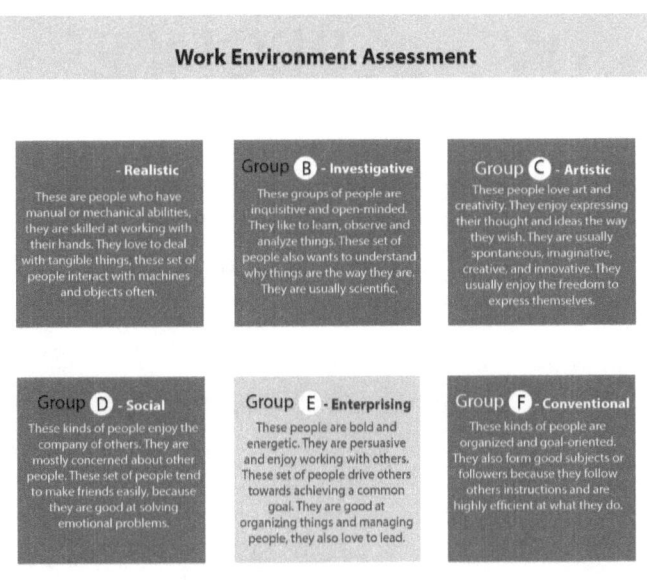

Figure 1.5.0 *Work environment assessment. Read the content in the table to discover the work environment that's right for you.*

According to the table above, list the group of people you would enjoy working with. You can either list with the title underneath the groups of your choice, or list with the name of the groups of your choice below.
_____For example: You can list using either of the methods

a. **Group A, Group B, Group C, Group D, Group F**
b. **Investigative**, **artistic**, **social**, and **enterprising**

Note: This assessment was adapted from Holland's codes of typology (J.L. Holland (1997)).

1.6 BUILDING YOUR WORK PROFILE

You have done different assessments, now it is time for you to re-visit all your answers and then use them to build your career profile. In this assessment, you will fill in the answers to the questions that you are asked. You can check your answers in previous assessments to be sure you are giving the right answer.
Values

What are the top 5 values I need to thrive in the workplace?

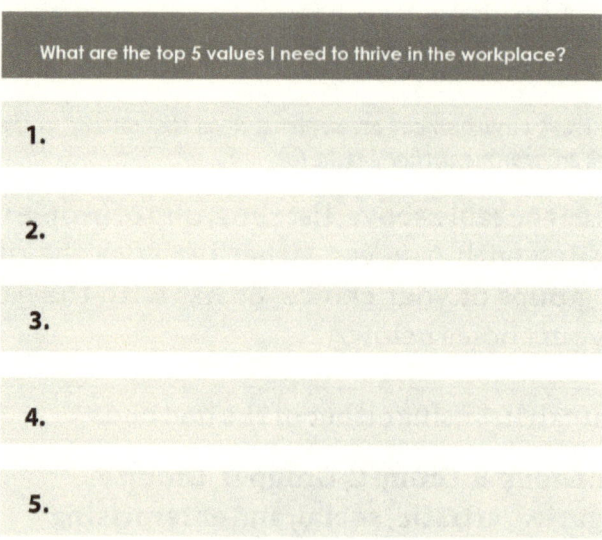

Figure 1.6.0 *Values you need to thrive in the workplace. Write down the workplace*

values you need in the table above.

Interests

What are the top 5 things I love/would love to do?

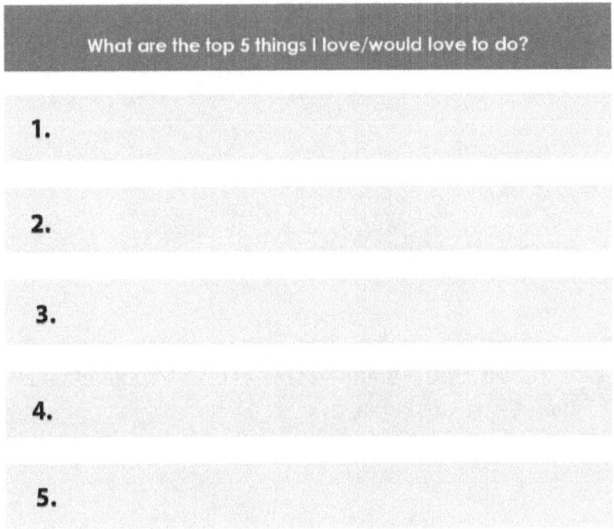

Figure 1.6.1 *Discovering your interest. Write down the things you love to do in the table above.*

Skills

What are the top 5 skills I would need to work efficiently?

What are the top 5 skills I would need to work efficiently?
1.
2.
3.
4.
5.

Figure 1.6.2 *Finding out your top skills. Write down the top skills you would need to work in the table above.*

Work Environment

What kind of people would I prefer to work with?

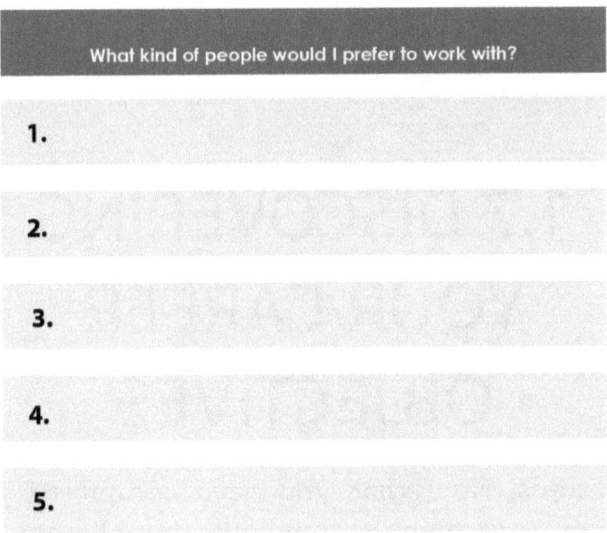

Figure 1.6.3 *Work environment assessment. Write down the group of people you would love to work with in the table above.*

1.7 DISCOVERING YOUR CAREER OBJECTIVES

Congratulations! Now that you have completed your self-examination assessment throughout this chapter, you will have a clearer idea of the kind of job that you would love to do.

Now, it is more like you know the career area you want to work in. Whether you want to work in a bank or a manufacturing company, now you can decide.

Use the ideas from all the assessments you have done so far and the ones in your work profile to create your career objectives.

Examples of some general career objectives are given below, so you can have a better understanding as to how you are going to form your own list.

General career objectives

- An entry-level position in an accounting or auditing company.
- A writing position in a media company.
- A research position in a chemical/oil & gas company.

You can use this method to write down your top 5 general career objectives in the space below:

Top 5 general career objectives
1.
2.
3.
4.
5.

Figure 1.7.0 *Discovering your career objectives. Write down your top career objectives in the table above.*

After you have filled in all the 5 spaces above, take time to go through what you have written and pick the top 2. This will give you an idea of the kind of job that you want to do.

Top 2 career objectives

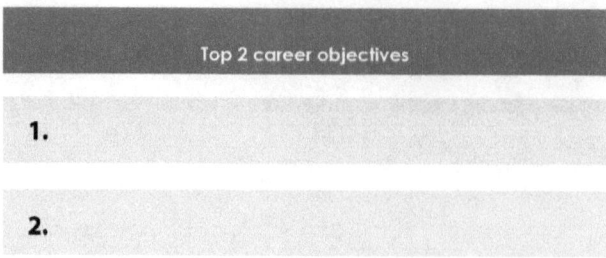

Figure 1.7.1 *Discovering your career objectives. Write down your top 2 career objectives in the table above.*

1.8 CHAPTER SUMMARY

The essence of this chapter is to help you discover yourself as regards your career path and also to help you figure out the jobs that you would love to do. If you have carefully gone through the assessments in this chapter, then you would have an idea of where your career is tending towards.

The next chapter will successfully guide you on the things you have to know before you even start searching for a job.

We are happy to see that you have successfully examined and discovered yourself as regards your career. Congratulations!

CHAPTER 2

CAREER RESEARCH (UNDERSTANDING THE WORLD OF WORK)

Congratulations! You have been able to examine yourself, discover who you are, and understand the career that best fits you. You have been able to discover yourself, so what next?

The whole process of searching for a job doesn't just start and end with you, it is necessary you understand what you are going into. After your self-examination, the next thing is for you to understand the "world of work".

It is almost impossible for you to land a job without understanding how the job search process works, what employers want, current trends, outdated practices, etc. All of which forms the world of work, it is important for you to know that different things work in different places. The American world of work will be different from the world of work in Nigeria, so what works in Nigeria may likely not work in America. This is why understanding what works where you are is key.

Regardless of where you are, knowing the latest job search trends and updates will go a long way to ensuring that you start your job search on the right foot. Understanding the world of work and doing a good research before you start your job search will help you find out the following:

- What job search method works?
- What employers want from employees?
- What options does the job market have for you?

·   What opportunities are available for you and how can you grasp the opportunities?

·   How do you know the skills and qualifications that employers want?

These are questions that you would likely answer after you have discovered who you are and what you would love to do. There is no problem if you don't have answers to the above questions.

This chapter will help you understand all you need to know about the world of work. The assessment exercises in this chapter will guide you on how and what you should research.

2.1 THE WORLD OF WORK

We have been talking about the 'world of work' and why it is important to understand it, but wait a minute, do you even know what the world of work means? Maybe you don't.

Just like we live in a world, everything that has to do with employment and the factors involved are all categorized in a world.

Okay, let's make this clear. We know the world to mean the earth (where all the people and countries and everything that makes up the earth live). On the other hand, work includes; employers, employees, compensation, etc. So considering the two terms world and work, what does the world of work mean to you? The world of work basically includes everything that has to do with work. It includes every aspect of employment and employment practices.

Now that you have an idea of what the world of work is, the next question is how does it affect me? Well, knowing what works in the world of work will determine how well you will thrive in it.

Before we talk about different factors that can help you thrive in the world of work, it is good we introduce you to the world of work in Nigeria.

2.2 WHAT IS THE WORLD OF WORK LIKE FOR JOB SEEKERS IN NIGERIA?

If you live in Nigeria, then the problem of youth unemployment should be no news. According to the report from the National Bureau of Statistics, the unemployment situation has risen to 23.1% in the third quarter of 2018. This simply means that a total of 20.9 million Nigerians who are willing and able to work don't have anything to do. *Surprised right?*

You may want to ask; if these number of people are unemployed, then why are they unemployed with all the information available. Looking at the Nigerian job market, different factors contribute to unemployment.

These are some of the factors that lead to unemployment in Nigeria:

- The population of people actively searching for jobs is far more than the available jobs, thereby resulting in a tense and competitive job market.
- There are more hidden jobs than open jobs (jobs that are advertised). One quarter of the available jobs in Nigeria is hidden, leaving the remaining for millions of job seekers to hustle for.
- According to MyJobMag survey, many job seekers

lack the necessary skills that employers are looking for. Many job seekers in Nigeria are not exposed to useful information that will guide them on how they can access jobs in Nigeria's competitive job market.

- Many job seekers in Nigeria are not exposed to useful information that will guide them on how they can access jobs in Nigeria's competitive job market.

The job market in Nigeria is an employer's job market, because millions of job seekers are chasing few jobs. This kind of situation puts employers in advantaged positions where they call the shot.

Looking at employment trends in Nigeria and different job seekers' survey, the following conclusions were made as to how job seekers can find jobs in Nigeria's competitive job market:

- Building a network of people that can connect you to job opportunities.

- You should have in-demand skills that employer want badly.

- Leave yourself to fate and accept any job that may later come your way regardless of what kind of job it is.

Now that you know what the world of work in Nigeria is like, so what now? There may be one question that you would love to ask, which is: If this is what the world of work feels like in Nigeria, are there any options for me? Yes, there are lots of options for you here in Nigeria. Before we talk about how you can get a job in Nigeria which we will talk about in subsequent chapters, let's focus on how you can research your career.

For now, we will focus on how you can research your career, understanding the world of work. Since you have an understanding of what the Nigerian job market feels like, it is now time for us to see how you can research the job market. This will help you discover what opportunities are there for you and how you can leverage those opportunities.

How do you start your research? You will weigh your career options by researching the following:

- Different employers/organizations.
- Different occupations.
- Different industries.
- Different job roles.
- Different job fields.

Researching the following will help you have a more focused job search because this way you are sure of what is available and what best fits your interests.

Before we go into the assessments for this exercise, we are going to first understand what all these mean and the different categories under them.

2.3 RESEARCHING EMPLOYERS/ ORGANIZATIONS

An employer is a person, institution or organization that employs workers. An employer is also a legal entity that controls and directs a worker under an express or implied contract of employment and pays them. (*businessdictionary.com*)

There are different types of employers. We are going to be looking at types of employers based on size and sector.

Types of Employers by Size

Different employers will be open to you when you are searching for a job, so you have to decide if you would like to work for a large company or start with an SME?
Now, we are going to take a quick look at the difference between the two.

Working for a Large Company

Just like you, every job seeker would love to work for large and well-known multinational companies because of the different things you hear they offer. Large companies are usually forthcoming with their job adverts and graduate programmes.

Just before you make that decision, you to know what it feels like to work for a large company. These are some of the benefits you are likely to get when you work for a large company:

- Competitive compensation and benefit package.
- Clear career path and progression within the organization.
- Planned career development programmes to help you build your career.
- Structured training programmes to aid your performance on the job.

A few disadvantages are:

- What you end up doing in your role/task may be below what you had envisioned initially.
- Relating what you do to the company's vision or goal can be quite challenging.
- It may be difficult for you to be noticed for your effort as a result of hierarchy.

Working for an SME

SMEs are businesses that employ fewer than 250 people. Most times, SMEs tend to be new, small and growing businesses. SMEs run in various sectors ranging from manufacturing, IT, etc.

Many fresh graduates will often not love to work for an SME, probably because their eyes are fixed on the 'Big Four' companies. Even if working for an SME may not have been your dream, there may be certain things you may not have been aware of.

These are some of the advantages you will likely be open to if you decide to work for an SME:

- You will likely gain experience in different aspects of the business.
- You will get real hands-on experience on the job.
- It is easier for you to get recognized for your effort.
- It is less hierarchical, so it is easy for you to bond with other staff members.
- Your salary can rise quickly as you get entrenched into the work system.

Some of the disadvantages of working for an SME may include:

- You may need to prove yourself quickly in a smaller company.
- Your actions will quickly have to show that you can actually contribute to the overall growth of the company. This can be checked even from your first 90 days at work.
- Job security can be quite low in smaller companies.
- Career growth and development may not be easily achieved in a small company.

Types of Employers by Sectors

When we talk about employers by sector, you should know that organizations/employers exist under different sectors. The major sectors for employment in Nigeria is; the private, public and the Non-profit sector (NGOs).

Getting into the world of work, knowing the sector that you would love to work in would go a long way to influence your career choice at the end of the day. Even if all the sectors are run as business a organization, the major difference between the sectors is; the work culture, the work environment, and of course the values which differ to a large extent. Keeping all these aspects in mind will help you to research better for your potential employers.

Working in the Private Sector

The private sector or organizations are businesses that are run to make profits, while there may still be other underlining aims and visions. Many times, private businesses achieve this by ensuring cost reduction and emphasizing revenue maximization.

Compensation structures in private sectors vary based on the profit that the company makes. Private businesses are run by private individuals. While many people don't admire the private sector, others do because most of the multinational companies belong to the private sector.

Working in the Public Sector

The public sector/organization are businesses that are controlled by the government and not individuals. These include organizations that are owned by the government. Many graduates look forward to working in the public sector because of work security, and other reasons.

Working in the Non-Profit Sectors

A non-profit organization operates differently from private and public businesses. These organizations are granted tax-exempt status by the revenue service because it propels a social cause and emphasizes public benefits.

If you are going to be working in the non-profit sector, these are basic features you should know:
· Non-profit organizations are established to address social or economic issues and not sell a product or service.
· They don't exist to generate revenue.
· They are usually not under any political control.
· Volunteers will make up the total population of staff members.
If you decide to work under the non-profit sector, you should be ready not to earn much because the organization doesn't make so much money.

Now that you understand the different types of employers, it is time for you to research the employer to determine the following:
· If your values match with that of the employer.
· If your skills will be better harnessed with the employer.
· If you would be happy working for the cause that the company is working for.

Researching an employer/organization may not be an easy thing to do, but asking the right questions will help you discover if a particular employer is right for you or not.

These questions will guide your research:

- What kind of employer/organization is it (public, private or non-profit)?
- What type of organization is it, based on size (is it a large company or an SME)?
- What is the goal of this organization and how do I fit into this goal?
- What product/service does this organization provide, and would I love to be a part of this?
- What kind of opportunities is open for me in this organization?
- What is the organization interested in when it comes to hiring a talent?

These questions will guide your research and help give your research a focus and a path. To guide you on your company research, we have put together this simple exercise.

Employer Research Exercise

Employers' Research Questions	Response
What type of organization is this? (Is it a private, public, or a non-profit organization).	
What is the size of this organization? (Is it a large organization or an SME).	
What do I need to thrive in this organization (what relevant skills can I acquire to thrive).	
Which organization(s) is/are this employer in competition with?	
What opportunities are open for me in this organization?	

Figure 2.3.0 *Employer research. Use the table above to discover the employer of your choice.*

You can go back to your answers on previous exercises to respond to some of the questions in this exercise. After filling the blank spaces above, you must have had an idea on the kind of employer you would like to work for.
You will write down the kind of employer that you would love to work for here.

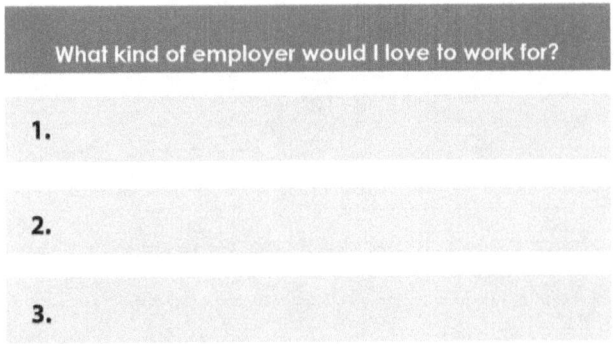

Figure 2.3.1 *Discovering your employer. Using the information in figure 2.3.0, write down your choice employer.*

Now that you have an idea of the kind of employers you would love to work for, it is time for you to take the next step; which is to further evaluate your employer option to see which is best for you.

This next exercise will help you further evaluate the decisions you have made from the exercise above. In this exercise, you will write down the advantages and disadvantages of your different employer options.

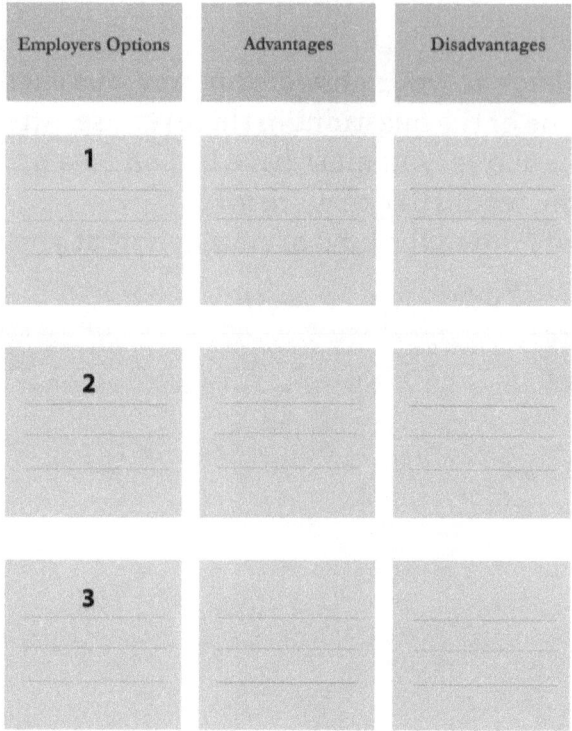

Figure 2.3.2 *Researching your employer. Write down the advantages and disadvantages of your choice employer to research properly.*

After this exercise, you would notice that your employer options have reduced from 3 to may be 1 or 2. Now you know the kind of employer that you would love to work for.

Write down the kind of employer that you would love to work for below:

The kind of employer I would love to work for?
1.
2.

Figure 2.3.3 *Finding out your employer. Write down the employer you would love to work for in the table above.*

2.4 RESEARCHING INDUSTRIES

Once you have researched the kind of employer that you would love to work for and discovered the organization, the next step is for you to research the industry.

For example, if I have discovered that I would love to work for a Private SME in Lagos, now the next thing for me to do is to discover what industry I will best function in right?

Before you research the industry that you will most likely fit into, it is good you understand what an industry is and the available different types. So, what is an industry?

When we talk about an industry, we are talking about all the activities by individuals and organizations that are involved in the production of goods and services for a particular field. So, we can say that a group of smart phones makers can be classified as an industry because they produce a common good.
Industries are classified into four groups:
- Primary industry
- Secondary industry
- Tertiary industry
- Quaternary industry

Primary industry

A primary industry is an industry that is involved in the extraction of natural resources, as well as activities such as farming and fishing. Primary industries are involved in transforming natural resources into products.

If you are still not clear about what a primary industry is, then take a look at the examples of the primary industry:

- Fishing
- Farming
- Quarrying
- Grazing
- Hunting
- Forestry

Secondary industry

Secondary industry is an industry sector that focuses on the manufacturing of finished products. While primary industries focus on processing raw materials for manufacture, secondary industries are concerned with processing raw materials to finished or usable products.

This means that this industry sector makes goods that are more likely to be used by consumers.

These are some examples of secondary industries:

- Manufacturing industry.
- Fast-moving consumer goods (FMCG)
- Construction industry.
- Food industry.
- Fashion industry.

Tertiary industry

The tertiary industry is an industry that provides goods and services to consumers using raw materials from the primary and secondary industries. Tertiary industry does not produce or manufacture goods, but they provide services.

- Telecommunication
- Hospitality industry/tourism
- Mass media
- Healthcare/hospitals
- Public health

- Pharmacy
- Information technology
- Waste disposal
- Consulting
- Gambling
- Retail sales
- Fast-moving consumer goods (FMCG)
- Franchising
- Real estate
- Education
- Financial services
- Banking
- Insurance
- Investment management
- Professional services
- Accounting
- Legal services
- Management consulting
- Transportation

Quaternary industry

The quaternary industry is a sector that is characterized by the knowledge base that the sector contributes to the economy. This industry is basically referred to as the knowledge-oriented sector. The quaternary sector is based on pure knowledge and skill of a person.

Examples of this industry include:

- Information technology.
- Media.
- Research.
- Financial services.
- Vocational education.
- Business consulting etc.

Since you now understand what an industry is and the different types of industries, it is time for you to take some assessments to help you research the industries that you will likely fit into. This exercise will help you discover what you want in a particular industry.

Research Questions	Response
What kind of industry is this?	
What opportunities are there for me in this industry?	
What kind of people work in this industry?	
What are the future trends in this job?	
What are the characteristics of people in this industry?	
What occupations are in this industry?	

Figure 2.4.0 *Researching industries. Use the table above to research the industry you would love to work in.*

2.5 RESEARCHING OCCUPATIONS

Before we start researching different occupations, you need to understand what an occupation means and the different types of occupations.

Generally, an occupation refers to the economic activities that are undertaken to earn money. When people engage in such activities regularly, then it is said to be their occupation.

Occupations are classified into the following categories:
- Profession
- Employment
- Business

Profession

A profession refers to an occupation that requires specialized training and knowledge to pursue. Every profession requires special knowledge to be acquired through training. For example, a medical doctor must have acquired a certain form of knowledge through training to be able to diagnose a patient.

Different professions are regulated by professional bodies to ensure professionals follow certain rules and practices. The aim of every profession is to provide services.

Employment

Employment is an occupation that a person does regularly for another person in order to get a wage or salary at the end of the stipulated period.

This does not mean that the person must work for another individual; the person can work for the government, community, or a private individual. In employment, there are usually terms and conditions as regards the job/task the person is to perform.

Sometimes, a professional can also be under an employment. Government workers, bank officials, etc. are examples of employments

Business

Business refers to an occupation where goods and services are produced to satisfy the wants of customers. In a business, goods and services are produced in exchange for money. Businesses run on a regular basis with the objective of making profit.
Manufacturing, trading, transporting, e-commerce, etc. are all examples of businesses.
Now that you have an idea of what an occupation is, then it is time for us to look at how you can research the particular occupation that is good for you.

Researching occupations exercise

There are many aspects for you to consider when it comes to researching the occupation that is right for you. When you are researching different occupations to discover the one that is right for you, you need to pay attention to the following:
- Your values
- Your interest
- Your experience
- Your skills
- Abilities
- Personality characteristics

Having these four factors in mind will guide you throughout the research. These factors will also form the basis for the questions that you would likely ask to find out the occupation that is best for you.

Don't forget to re-visit your career assessment response in
Since you have created a job profile in the previous chapter, it is
good to ask yourself some of these questions to determine the
occupation that is right for you:

- What is this occupation like?
- What skills are required in this occupation?
- What educational training is required to progress in
  this occupation?
- Are there opportunities for advancement in this occupation?
- What are the common values held in this occupation; do these values match with my values?
- What is the salary range or benefits in this occupation, does it match with my needs and lifestyle?
- What kind of personality thrives in this career?
- What kind of working conditions should I look forward to in this occupation?
- Are there professional bodies or associations regulating practices and policies in this occupation?
- Are there other related positions I should be exploring within this occupation?

These questions will guide you on the information you should
be focused on getting when you are researching your occupation.

You probably have some occupation options on your mind; to
help you pen your decisions down so that they appear even
more tangible, we have created this assessment for you. Excited
right? Let's get into it!

First, you are going to list 5 occupations that you are interested
in below:

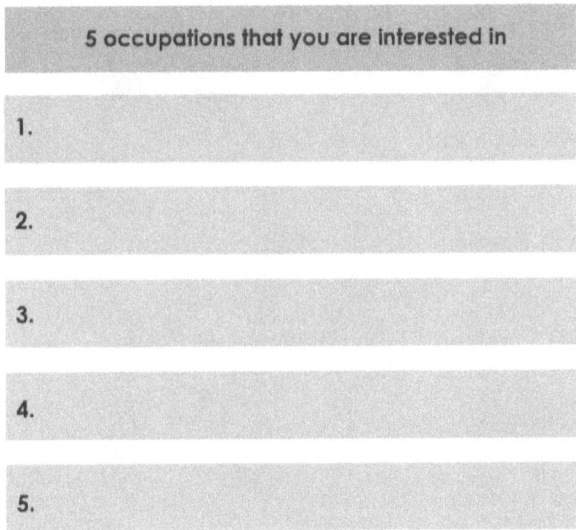

Figure 2.5.0 *Researching your occupation. Write down your occupation of interest in the table above.*

Organizational Research Questions	Response
Which occupation do you want to research?	
What are the duties and responsibilities in this occupation?	
What skills are required in this occupation?	
Are there opportunities for advancement in this occupation?	
What are the common values held in this occupation, do these values match with my values?	
What is the salary range or benefits in this occupation, does it match with my needs and lifestyle?	
What kind of personality thrives in this career?	
What kind of working conditions should I look forward to in this occupation?	
Are there professional bodies or associations regulating practices and policies in this occupation?	
Are there other related positions I should be exploring within this occupation?	

Figure 2.5.1 *Occupational research assessment. Respond to questions in the table above to discover the occupation that is right for you.*

Finally, you have gotten to the end of this chapter. Don't forget the title of this chapter which is 'researching careers'. At the end of this chapter, you are supposed to have a clear idea of the kind of career that you would love to pursue and develop.

If you are still confused about the career choice you should make, then this exercise will help you make your final decision.

Career research exercise

In this exercise, you are going to write down 5 advantages and disadvantages of your career option in the spaces below:

My career option is --------------------

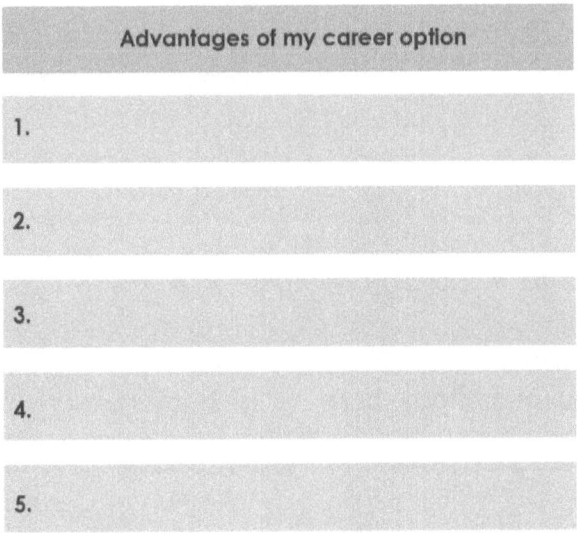

Figure 2.5.2 *Career option research. Write down the advantages of your career option in the table above.*

Disadvantages of my career options
1.
2.
3.
4.
5.

Figure 2.5.3 *Career option research. Write down the disadvantages of your career choice.*

Write your career choice here

2.6 CHAPTER SUMMARY

Congratulations! You now understand the world of work, the things to look forward to, and most importantly how you fit into this world. You may not be aware of it, but you have taken a great step, and you are just a few steps away from landing your dream job.

The essence of this chapter is to help you understand the world of work and to also help you research your career. If you have carefully gone through this chapter, then you have a good understanding of the job market and how you fit in.

We are extremely happy that you understand the job market now, and your career options. We would love to see your progress in other chapters.

CHAPTER 3

FINDING A JOB (HOW TO FIND A JOB)

We know the job market does not look favourable. It is no longer news that about 20.9 million Nigerians are unemployed. This information can be quite terrifying especially if you are new to job search. Looking at the situation of things in the Nigerian job market, you can't help but ask yourself these questions:

- What is the best way for me to start searching for a job?
- How will I know companies that are interested in me?
- Can I ever find a job, and if it is possible, how do I go about achieving it?

As a fresh graduate trying to find a job, there are many things you are probably confused about. It is completely normal to feel quite confused when you are doing something that you have not done before (which is job search in this case).

Even if you are new to job search, you don't have to be scared about finding a job. Searching for a job is simply like searching for any other thing, while some searches are blind, others are effective. So how can someone search effectively?

To search effectively, you have to:
- Know what you are searching for.
- Know where to search.

If you have been able to establish these two things, then chances are that you will have an effective search. Since we are talking about how to find a job, and then let's focus on 'job search'. So if you want your job search to be effective, it is important you:

- Get it together (discover yourself).
- Get hold of what employers want.
- Pin-point what you can offer.
- Find out the career that best suits you.

If this is what it takes to have an effective job search, guess what... you are on the right path! You know why? It is simple. If you have carefully read chapter 1 and 2 of this book and have taken all the assessments/exercises, then you can rest assured that your job search is effective because you have discovered yourself, known what you can offer, and found out the careers that best suit you.

In this chapter, we are going to look at how you can find a job in this competitive job market.

3.1 UNDERSTANDING THE JOB MARKET

Yes, the job market is tense and extremely competitive, but what works despite the competition? Regardless of what's happening in the job market, just know that there is a way around everything. Look at it this way; if some people are still getting jobs despite the situation, then how do they go about it?

Looking at the world of work, there are some things that you have probably not known yet. The fundamental truth about the job market is that there are more jobs than you know. Surprised?

According to Forbes, 70% - 80% of jobs are not posted online. Since these jobs are not posted where you would see them, so where are they? This is why they are referred to as "hidden jobs"

The next question is; how do hidden jobs even exist or why do hidden jobs even exist. Hidden jobs exist because of the following reasons:

- No one has advertised the job vacancy online or on the newspaper where people will probably see it.
- Companies prefer hiring through referrals or prefer to promote existing staff members to vacant positions instead of hiring new staff members.
- Some companies prefer to hide their jobs to save the cost of posting jobs.
- Some top companies want to avoid screening a large number of CV's, so they decide to make their job vacancies private by hiding the jobs.

By now, you should have understood the job market to an extent. In our discussion on the job market two things stood out, do you know what they are:

a.   So many people are unemployed.

b.   There are more hidden jobs than advertised jobs.

Since you have discovered that there are many hidden jobs than advertised jobs, the question you might be asking yourself is; is it possible for me to access hidden jobs, and even if it is possible, how can I do it?

- Yes! you can access hidden jobs.
- Secondly, hidden jobs are primarily accessed through networking.

According to research, the best possible way to access hidden jobs is through networking. Since networking is the secret to accessing hidden jobs, how then can you network?

Before we talk about how you can network to land a job, you need to understand what networking means.

3.2 WHAT IS NETWORKING?

Networking is getting to know people. The funny thing about networking is that whether you know it or not, you are networking every day and everywhere you go. You want to know how?

You are networking when you initiate a conversation with the person sitting close to you on the bus, meeting up with a former classmate, or even stopping to chat with your neighbour. Anyone can help move your career forward.

Yes! Networking is this simple, but you can't always depend on accidental networking to land your dream job. To leverage networking to access the hidden job market, you have to be deliberate to network professionally.

3.3 WHY DO YOU HAVE TO NETWORK PROFESSIONALLY?

A research carried out by Jobvite revealed that *60% of employers' best candidates came through referrals*. This reveals how employers find candidates and that is one of the reasons why you should network professionally. Networking deliberately opens you up to opportunities that you did not expect.

Networking professionally will also help you track your efforts and measure your results. In the next section, we are going to be talking about steps to take to network professionally.

3.4 HOW TO NETWORK PROFESSIONALLY

a. Attend professional events and conferences

Professional events like meet-ups, seminars and conferences provide a great opportunity for people to network. Attending professional events allows you to meet and network with like-minded people and even people that are even more experienced than you are. Professional events are great avenues for you to network because they bring professionals together, create an atmosphere of people with a common goal, and makes it is easy for you to network because you already have a basic understanding of what the next person is interested in. In this kind of event, it is easy for you to strike a conversation about your career goals with the person sitting next to you.

b. Attend casual meet-ups with people in your field

From bars, to restaurants or gardens, a meet-up may not look like the place to network professionally, but this can be a great way to network with other people in your career field or the career field that you would love to go into. Most times, it is more effective to discuss professional stuff like your career goals and job search concerns in a relaxed and fun environment. Meeting up with a professional in a bar eases the tension and makes both parties comfortable with the discussion, unlike the tense and intimidating environments in professional events.

c. Engage with others on professional Facebook groups

Joining Facebook groups is a great way for you to network, and why is that? It is convenient plus it prevents the awkward feeling of having to start a conversation physically with someone that you just met. Networking on Facebook groups is easy, because it doesn't require much of your efforts. All you need to do is simply, search for groups that you may be interested in on Facebook, then join. Once you have joined the group, be sure to engage regularly with other members to start building connections and also building your reputation with the groups. Contributing effectively in the group and asking intelligent questions will help you stand out in the groups.

d. Join alumni groups

Sharing a common idea or value like an Alma mater makes it easy for you to start and build a great connection. Finding your alumni group is quite easy; you can search for your alumni group on Facebook. Once you have found your alumni group, try to reach out to people on the group especially those that are working in companies that you would love to work in.

e. Get active on LinkedIn

Getting active on LinkedIn can help you network effectively. LinkedIn has a lot of features that are great for networking. Keeping up with your LinkedIn page like; updating your profile, getting endorsements, etc. is important, but you can take an extra step to make connections with other people in your field. If you are just in the journey to discovering your career path, you can search for the particular job field that you would love, search for people in that field and then connect with them.

f. Reach out to industry professionals

It can appear difficult and intimidating to reach out to industry professionals, because you may feel like they may not respond to you. Professionals are mostly interested in an enthusiastic job seeker.

Reaching out to professionals is easy, you just have to make sure you start the conversation on good ground and also ask intelligent questions when necessary. Employers and professionals get irritated when you are trying to be unnecessarily familiar and informal. You can send a professional email or LinkedIn message to a professional and tell them how you admire what they do and how you are also passionate and would love to learn more about what they do.

g. Always keep up and share your career goals

It could be somehow funny how what you are searching for can just be right under your nose. While you are trying to network, don't forget to keep up with family members, friends, and even old classmates.

You can do this by getting in touch with friends, family members and colleagues during lunch or over a cup of coffee. Always remember to congratulate others for their recent accomplishments and life events. Staying relevant on social media platforms can also make it easy for you to bond with family and friends.

h. Seek professional advice

Professional advice is necessary for your career growth and development. You don't have to worry if you don't know anyone that can give you the professional advice that you need, it is quite easy to get professional advice if you are open to it.

Getting a career mentor is a great way to access career advice. Once you have a career mentor, you can be free to open up to the person about your career challenges. Your mentor can guide you on the right path to go to achieve your career goals. When you are trying to get a career mentor, don't expect that the person will help you find a job. The essence of the mentorship is for guidance. Even if your mentor can help you get a job, don't abuse that opportunity, let it come from them willingly.

You don't need to be confused about where you can find mentors, because it is quite easy to find one. You can find a career mentor on LinkedIn or during professional events like career fairs, seminars, conferences, etc. You can get better guidance when you find a mentor in your field.

Okay, we have spent some time talking about the hidden job market and how you can access jobs in the hidden job market, which is basically through networking. We have also seen how networking can be a great way for you to access more jobs, and also how you can network effectively.

Well, if you have mastered all the networking channels, what about how you can start a conversation with a potential employer when a networking opportunity pops up? It is almost useless if you attend all the networking events and you are not even able to strike a conversation with anybody. So, in the next section, we are going to focus on how you can start a great conversation when you are in a networking environment.

3.5 THE BEST WAY TO START A CONVERSATION DURING NETWORKING AND TOP 20 QUESTIONS TO ASK

Starting a conversation during a networking event could feel a bit awkward, because you are probably meeting these people for the first time, and so you still feel uncomfortable. Regardless of how you feel, you can't deny yourself the opportunity of networking with great people that might help you move your career to the next level.

So, if you were finally able to be in a networking environment, it won't be nice for you to ruin this opportunity because you don't know how to start a conversation. To prevent this from happening, we have put these tips together to guide you on how to start a conversation in a networking event. These tips are what you need to start networking on the right foot:

a. Be approachable
When you are in a networking event, don't hide in a corner

scrolling social media notifications on your phone like you don't care about anyone. Well, if you don't care about talking to anyone, then you should not be at a networking event.

No matter how shy you are, the fact remains that you are at a networking event and you have to fulfill your purpose. Even if you are really shy of talking to people first, you can attract people to talk to you by putting on an approachable outlook.

Make sure you are not frowning, do your best to keep a light face. Don't be scared to smile when someone looks towards your direction.

b. Sustain a great outlook with your actions

During a networking event, there is a probability that someone might walk up to you to start a conversation. When people walk up to you to start a conversation, make sure you sustain the conversation with your actions.

How can you sustain a great outlook with your actions? One of the ways you can sustain a great outlook is by:

      a. Having a great handshake when you introduce yourself.
      b. Keeping eye contact.
      c. Smiling and keeping a light face.

c. Begin with a question

Asking a question is always a great way to start a conversation in a networking event. According to research, asking a question is a great way to build rapport and to also a way to show that you interested in other people. If you are with a group of people in a networking event and you are stuck as to how you can start a conversation with them, try asking them any of the questions below:

Questions that will help you know them

      a. What do you do?
      b. How did you discover this is what you love to

do?

c. For how long have you been doing this?

d. What do you like most about what you do?

e. What is the biggest project you have worked on doing this job?

f. What do you love most about your job?

Questions that will help you understand their job field

a. What kind of education is required to get into this field?

b. What skills do you think someone getting into this field needs to acquire?

c. What activities do you engage in to develop your career?

d. What advancement can you say this field has made over the years?

e. Where do you see this field in like 10 years?

Questions that will help you find out more about their organization

a. For how long have you been with this organization?

b. What is this company's culture like?

c. What can you say has made your company stand out despite the competition?

d. What can you say is the biggest challenge that your company has faced?

e. Where can you say your company is headed in few years?

Questions that will help you wrap up the conversation

a. What is the next step you think you need to take in your career?

b. What is next for you in your career?

c. How can I help you achieve your goals?

d. Would you love to keep in touch?

We have come a long way with networking and how you can find a job through networking, now it's time for you to take some assessments and exercise to guide you on how you can network.

Before, you go-ahead to take the assessment, you have to fill this sheet to discover your network. All you have to do is to write your response to these questions below:

Discovering your network

People I knew from School

My classmates

a. _____
b. _____
c. _____
d. _____

My Lecturers

a. _____
b. _____
c. _____
d. _____

Alumni members

a. _____
b. _____
c. _____

d. _____

Figure 3.5.0 *Discovering your network. Use the table above to discover your network.*

People I know personally

Family members

a. _____
b. _____
c. _____
d. _____

Friends

a. _____
b. _____
c. _____
d. _____

Neighbours

a. _____
b. _____
c. _____
d. _____

Church members

a. _____
b. _____
c. _____
d. _____

Figure 3.5.1 *Discovering your network. Use the table above to discover your network.*

People I know from work

Colleagues

a. _____
b. _____
c. _____
d. _____

Employers

a. _____
b. _____
c. _____
d. _____

Supervisors

a. _____
b. _____
c. _____
d. _____

Customers

a. _____
b. _____
c. _____
d. _____

Figure 3.5.2 *Discovering your network. Use the table above to discover your network.*

People I knew randomly

Connections I made at career fair

a. _____
b. _____
c. _____
d. _____

Connections I made at a conference

a. _____
b. _____
c. _____
d. _____

Friends I met at a community meeting

a. _____
b. _____
c. _____
d. _____

Figure 3.5.3 *Discovering your network. Use the table above to discover your network.*

After you have filled this form, you would have discovered the major areas and the different people that makes up your network. Knowing your network and your potential network is the first step to networking effectively.

This next exercise will help you examine your networking skill and also discover areas you need to develop on. Let's get into the exercise.

Networking Self-Assessment Questions	Self Rating (1 - 5)	Assessments
I often ask friends to provide feedback on my approach for dealing with situations.		
I have no problem approaching people about new ideas.		
When trying to take a decision, I determine who in my network to contact.		
I send friends links to posts and articles that might interest them.		
I frequently ask mentors for advice regarding work related problems.		
I am comfortable taking the lead in a meeting.		
Before starting out on a project, I find out what information is needed and how I can provide it.		
I invest my time and effort maintaining my network of colleagues.		
I write thank-you messages to my contact after they have helped me.		
I love initiating conversations with people that I have never met before.		
I periodically organize my contact list to focus on people who have assisted		
I am good at taking steps to make myself known to influential people in my field.		
I use social networking tools (e.g. LinkedIn, Face book, Twitter)		
I am good at identifying people outside my organization who have valuable information or insights.		
I am very comfortable displaying a lack of knowledge by asking a colleague for help.		
Immediately after I encounter difficult situations at work, I ask others for guidance about possible courses of action.		

Figure 3.5.4 *Networking self-assessment. The table above will help you discover your networking abilities.*

Scoring yourself assessment

In this exercise, you have to write down your scores from the previous exercise and then fill them in the spaces below. Calculate your scores based on the different categories in the table below and then calculate the total scores for each category.

Identifying Information/ Expertise and Who Can Provide It	Reaching Out	Asking for Help	Maintaining Relationships
3. ___	2. ___	1. ___	4. ___
7. ___	6. ___	5. ___	8. ___
11. ___	10. ___	16. ___	9. ___
14. ___	12. ___	15. ___	13. ___
Total:	Total:	Total:	Total:

Figure 3.5.5 *Networking self-assessment. Use the table to discover how good your networking skill is.*

After filling the spaces above, calculate your total scores for each category. Take note of the category where you scored the highest and category where you scored the lowest. Taking note of these details will help you know the areas where you need to improve on and areas that you are strong at.

This table will help you interpret your scores in relation to your networking skills.

Score Range	Meaning	Interpretation
9 or lower	Low than others	Potential growth area
10 – 15	Moderate/Average	Average
16 or higher	High	A strength to leverage

Figure 3.5.6 *Networking self-assessment. Use the table above to score your networking ability.*

The first step to finding a job is to first understand the job market and how you can thrive in it. So far, we have been able to understand that there are hidden jobs in the Nigerian market and the only way to access these jobs is through networking.

We have been able to understand what networking is and how you can network effectively. The assessments on networking will help you understand networking more.

3.6 FINDING A JOB ON THE INTERNET

There are indeed hidden jobs considering the job market. Although 60% - 80% of jobs are hidden, there are lots of advertised jobs that you can access online. When we even talk about finding a job on the internet, networking and the traditional method (newspaper) still plays a big role.

In today's job search, using the internet has become a necessity. It is almost impossible for you to search for a job in this 21st century without searching online. We know that the internet has invaded our lives and changed the way we see things. One of the changes that we would ever appreciate is the way the internet has helped us to search and apply for jobs. It couldn't have been easier.

Using the internet during your job search is inevitable whether you are finding job listings, connecting to contacts, researching companies, applying for jobs online or emailing your cover letters and resumes.

Not having access to the internet will make your job search challenging. So if you want to leverage the opportunities that are available in today's job market, you should get active on the internet.

No doubt, the internet is the right place to find and apply for advertised jobs and a great place to post your CV to reach millions of employers. Many job seekers and maybe you too are usually confused about how they can leverage the internet for their job search. Before we talk about how you can use the internet to search for a job, it is good you even understand why you should use the internet to search for a job in the first place.

3.7 WHY YOU SHOULD GO ONLINE IN THE FIRST PLACE

If you have used Facebook to reconnect with old friends and family, then you understand the thrills that come with discovering something new which is what the internet does for you. You might wonder how the internet is particularly useful for job search.

The internet is particularly useful for job search for the following reasons:

- The internet will enable you to have access to millions of job postings in all parts of the world.
- The internet allows you to search for jobs at any time and from anywhere.
- The internet will also allow you to discover opportunities that you may not have been open to initially.
- The internet will make it easy for you to network with people that you may not be able to meet with on a normal day.
- The internet helps you locate difficult-to-find career information.
- The internet helps you communicate with professionals and resource groups in your areas of interest.
- The internet makes it easy for you to research companies, organizations and agencies.

- The internet makes it easy for you to post your resume and apply for jobs online.

Once you get used to the process of using the internet to search for jobs, you would notice that it is easier than using the traditional method. All you need to do is to type a keyword or a string of keywords in the website's search space.

While using the internet to search for jobs is great, it is also good for you to be wise about it and apply some caution. Do you know why you should apply some caution? It is simply because if you don't apply a caution you may face some major drawbacks like:

- Too many confusing career and job search information.
- Privacy threat that may come as a result of posting your CV online.
- Over utilizing the internet while under utilizing other job search methods (People, events, etc.).
- Loss or disappearance of useful information.

With all the information that we have talked about when it comes to searching for a job online, you may want to ask; "How can I get a job online?" Well, getting a job online is not a difficult thing to do, because, with just a simple click, you have millions of job opportunities in front of you. Interesting right? Let's see how this works:

Job listing Platforms

The internet can be such an amazing aid to your job search, do you know why? It is because the internet can accelerate your job search by putting millions of job opportunities in front of you.
Job listing websites like myjobmag.com provides verified job listings for job seekers in Africa. You can only get few jobs listing using traditions means, but with the internet and the help of job listing sites the search is even easier.

Job listing platform makes it easy for you to access job vacancies that are specific to your needs rather than merely searching online. The services of job listings platforms make the job search journey less stressful.

One of the ways you can take advantage of job listing sites' services is to subscribe to their newsletters. Subscribing to their newsletters will enable you to get notified as soon as new opportunities show up. Using job listing sites can make your job search really interesting, don't forget to visit the site regularly or better still download their app if possible to get used to the features.

Social media

We know that almost everyone is on social media these days, but have you wondered how you can use social media to search and apply for jobs.

Just like how social media allows you to keep up with friends and even meet new people, social media can also help you get up close and personal with employers, friends and co-workers. For example; Twitter gives you the opportunity to follow employers and companies who offer information about job openings.
Just like Twitter, Facebook is also an amazing social media platform that can aid your job search. With thousands of corporate pages that gives useful information and even latest job listings, getting a job on Facebook has become a trend. Don't get carried away with your Facebook notifications and pop-ups. Facebook can provide an opportunity for you to land a job.

LinkedIn has become one of the most important tools when it comes to online networking. Asides the fact that you get the opportunity to see different job listings on LinkedIn, it will also enable you to access the hidden job market through networking.

Researching employers

One of the best ways to land a satisfying job is to track the employers of dreams and connect with them. Researching employers simply has to do with finding out useful information about the organization that you would love to work for.

The information should include; finding out about the company's vision, job vacancies, and work environment. Researching an employer will allow to find out many things about the company that you may not have discovered earlier.
When you want to research a company, LinkedIn can be a great tool for you to research employers and companies. LinkedIn allows you to narrow your search to specific reasons; you can view details of employers and determine if it is a company you would love to work for.

Researching Salaries

One of the reasons why many job seekers can't find jobs is because of their salary expectations; this is why it is important for you as a job seeker to have a reasonable expectation about your salary.

Several websites that can help you find out about necessary information you wish to get about salary information and how to go about salary negotiation. While the National Bureau of Statistics is a great place to search for information regarding salaries, other websites provides easy-to-use tools and information regarding salaries. mysalaryscale.com is one of the top salary research website that provides you with amazing tools. MySalaryScale will also help you know your worth and discover your market value for the job you are applying for.

Knowing your worth helps you stay in charge and in control of your negotiation and the entire job search process.

Presenting your CV

Searching for a job on the internet doesn't just have to do with searching for a job that you are interested in, but it also has a lot to do with telling your prospective employer that you are the best person out of everyone else that has applied for that same role.

So, how do you tell your prospective employer that you are the best person for the job? The best way to convince your prospective employer that you are the best person for the job is through your resume. The internet helps you showcase your CV to employers in a professional way.

Websites like Myjobmag.com makes it easier for jobseekers to create a professional CV themselves even if they have not done it before with the CV builder tool.

It is one thing to search for a job and it is another thing for employers to see your CV. The internet makes this combination possible.

Using search engines

The search engine can be a useful place to find jobs online. You can search for your favourite companies on the internet and create a connection for yourself. Connecting and networking with top companies that you wish to work for will eventually help you work your way to landing a satisfying job.

Since you understand that the internet is a great tool to help you accelerate your job search journey, we know you can't wait to jump right into it. Before you start sending out your CV you have to prepare. When we say prepare, what do we mean?

3.8 PREPARATION BEFORE USING THE INTERNET TO SEARCH FOR JOBS

Preparing to start searching for a job online does not require so much as you would imagine, it will require you to pay more attention to details more than you did normally if you want to get a result.

One of the things you want to make sure you have got right is your CV. You don't want to send out a CV that is below standard, because if you dare do that, your CV might end up being trashed and of course, your purpose defeated.

So what do you need to get together before you start applying all the steps to finding a job online?

a.   **Discover who you are:** Just like we stated earlier in chapter one, that you have to discover yourself because you are the most important factor in the scheme of things. Talking about who you are; you have to know what interests you, what environment you thrive in the most, what motivates you, etc.

b.   **Find out what you can do**: It is necessary for you to find out what you can do even before you start using the internet to search for a job. Even if you don't have a good grasp of what you can do, you should be able to find out what you want to do.

For example; are you a professional customer service executive? or do you like to serve under a project manager because you have discovered that your interests and skills will work better in project management?

c.   **Know the job field that interests you**: If you don't know the job field that interests you, you might likely have a vague job search that is neither here nor there. You must have a focus or an idea of what you want to effectively make use of the internet to find a job.

You should particularly know the job field that catches your interest. For example, you know that you would love to work in the medical field generally. This way you know that medicine is for you.

If you are at this point, at least you have an idea of what you want. This is what will make you have a focused job search. There are loads of jobs on the internet, so knowing what you want will help you streamline your job search.

d.   **Discover who you want to work for:** Talking about streamlining your job search, discovering the employer you want to work for goes a long way to streamline your job search even further. For example; do you look forward to working for an SME or a multinational organization due to some reasons best known to you?

e.   **Where do you want to work:** Another thing that you should consider when searching for a job is to know where you would love to work. Knowing where you want to work will add more specificity to your job search.

Employers also consider a job seeker's location as one of the criteria for deciding if the candidate will be a great fit for the job. It is also important for you to consider your location when you are searching for a job.

If you have carefully read the previous chapters of this book and followed the assessments, then you can beat your chest and say that you have got all the things that we listed above together. That is amazing, right?

Once you understand the process of searching for a job on the internet, then you will see that it is much easier to use the internet to search for a job than using other traditional means.

Once you have been able to put all these things together, and finally start searching for jobs on the internet, there is a very high possibility that you would get used to using some job sites. Before you endorse any job site, it is good you put up some form of check to ensure you get maximum result from your effort. Setting up a website is not much of a big deal these days, which means that anyone can own a website including "scammers".

To avoid falling into the hands of internet scammers, you should always know:

What the website offers

Before you commit yourself to a particular website, it is good you know what you are sure to get from the website. This can happen only if you understand what the website offers.

While some job sites offer just job listings, some offer other things like; networking opportunities, discussion groups, articles and newsletters with job-search tips, etc.

How frequently they post jobs

You need to check how frequent the site posts jobs . There are some sites that don't update their job listings regularly, if this is the case, then you may only see outdated jobs. A job site that updates their jobs regularly will make more opportunities open to you

Who runs the website

You can easily search for the person that runs the company by simply clicking the "About Us" link at the top or the bottom of the website. If you can't get any useful information about the company from the link, you can also search for the name of the company on Google to know a little more about the company.

While some websites are legitimate, others are owned by fraudsters.

What their customer service is like?
If you are going to spend time on any site, then make sure you get the assistance you desire. A website that is dedicated to adding value should be willing to assist their users and assist them in navigating the site.
Once you start using a website, send them an email and see how long it takes them to respond to your message.

What the company's privacy policy is
Some job websites make money by selling members' information to shady companies. To prevent this from happening, you need to take a look at the site's privacy policy. Checking a website privacy policy will help you know if your information is safe with that particular website or not.

Paying for features
Depending on what you want to achieve, websites offer paid features to job seekers. While some of these features are worth it, others are merely aimed at extorting their members. Many legitimate job websites will allow you make use of basic features for free.

If a job site is charging you for merely viewing listed jobs or reading a post, then there is a possibility that the website is not legitimate. Some shady websites may make you register just to view job listings. A trustworthy website should at least allow you to have basic experience of the site for free.

If you are new to job search and don't know where to start from, you can start by asking friends and family members about job search sites that are trustworthy. Create a list from there and then start your own research.

You can also search for top job website depending on your location on Google to have an idea of where to start from.

3.9 KEEPING RECORDS OF YOUR TIMELINE ONLINE

Once you are desperate, there is a high possibility that you would be tempted to send out hundreds of application every day.

Many job seekers apply for so many jobs that they even forget the company they applied to and the position they applied for when they are invited for an interview. As a job seeker, it is easy for you to forget the companies that you applied to and the position that you applied for if you don't keep a record of your activities. Tracking your job search activities will help you keep a record of companies that you have applied to and the different position you have applied for with the dates.

Before you start searching for a job each day, you should do the following:

a. **Get a note pad and a pen**
Getting a note pad and a pen will help you take notes and keep records of the sites that you are visiting for that day and the jobs you are applying for with the dates. You can also use any electronic device.

b. **Time yourself.**
Just scrolling through job listings can take a lot of time,

and at the end, yield little or no result at all. Timing yourself will help you calculate and budget a particular time for your online job search. This way you are not spending time scrolling; rather, you are having a calculated search.

c. Make sure your device is fully charged for the time that you would be using it.

Ensuring that your device is fully charged is also important. If your device goes off when you are in the middle of an activity, then it may not be easy for you to properly track your activities due to the interruption.

d. Create a calendar

There are other information and resources you will need to get from a job site asides the job listings. So, it is important for you to create a calendar that states which areas of your job search you are going to focus on each day.

Remember to add dates when creating your job search calendar. You can use this sample to create your own calendar:

Figure 3.9.0 *Job search calendar. Use the calendar above to keep track of your job search activities.*

Creating a calendar like this will help you keep track record of your online job search activities
I guess that by now, you have a great understanding of how searching for a job online works. If you just started using the internet to search for jobs, then it is good you check how well you are leveraging the internet for your job search.

Internet Use Assessment

In this section, you are going to take a simple assessment to access how well you use the internet for your job search.

Questions/Answers	Reasons
1. What kinds of jobs do I want to apply for?	
2. Companies I would love to work for?	
3. What Job website fit my needs?	
4. What Features do I need on a job site to make my search more effective?	
5. What other resources do I need to accelerate my job search?	

Figure 3.9.1 *Internet use assessment. Use the table above to assess how you use the internet for your job search.*

3.10 HOW TO USE LINKEDIN TO SEARCH FOR AND LAND A JOB

If you have been actively searching for jobs and you have not heard about LinkedIn, then where have you been?

It is no news that LinkedIn is the top professional social networking platform with millions of users reaching over 200 countries of the world. According to Jobvite survey, 87% of recruiters use LinkedIn as part of their candidate search tool.

Many job seekers are not utilizing LinkedIn for their job search because many of them merely see LinkedIn as an online CV (an online version of their regular CV). Is LinkedIn somehow like an online CV? Yes, LinkedIn can be considered as an online CV to an extent, but it is an online CV with a difference. It is different because unlike your regular online CV, it doesn't just sit there and wait for someone to view it. It is a platform where millions of employers are looking for top candidates each day. If this was a CV, don't you think it is a cool CV to have?

LinkedIn is an amazing platform that lets you network with employers and professionals in your field of interest without having to pass through the stress of meeting with them physically. Asides from networking with professionals, you can achieve a great amount of job search success with LinkedIn. You want to know how? Let's get started

Why you should use LinkedIn for your job search

Yes, you have heard many people say a lot of great stuff about LinkedIn, but you still don't understand why you should use LinkedIn for your job search. Okay, LinkedIn is a great social networking platform that exposes job seekers to lots of opportunities.

If you are not sure whether LinkedIn is the right platform for your job search, then these tips will convince you. LinkedIn is great for job seekers because it will help you:

a. Have access to thousands of job vacancies

LinkedIn can be more than just a social networking platform for you as a job seeker. With LinkedIn, you can get access to thousands of jobs in fields of your interest. With LinkedIn, you can search for jobs based on location or by even using keywords.

Using LinkedIn as a job board allows you some form of flexibility, with LinkedIn you can subscribe to get job alerts if you are not actively searching for a job (This allows you stay in the loop even if you are not actively searching).

LinkedIn allows you to inform recruiters that you are open to job opportunities if you have connected with co-workers and managers. You can do this by turning on your "I'm interested button" that will send alerts that you are open. With LinkedIn premium, you can access more job search information.

b. Build your brand

Just like companies build their brands, building a personal brand helps you stand out from every other person in your industry and also markets your skills and achievements to recruiters and prospective employers.

LinkedIn can help you build a professional brand without having to spend a lot of money and time to build a website and also optimizing it. With LinkedIn, you can put yourself and your career in the face of thousands of employers without spending a dime.

Using LinkedIn, you can put yourself in front of thousands of employers with a few clicks. All you have to do is to upload a professional profile picture and write a powerful summary that emphasizes your strength and showcases your brand.

c.   Research companies and employees

If you are actively searching for jobs, asides using the LinkedIn job board to see vacancies there are other ways you can get information about job vacancies.

A lot of companies use their LinkedIn pages to update their information and also showcase their company culture to attract prospective employees. LinkedIn also allows you research companies you would love to work for and follow up with them to keep abreast of information.

Asides from researching a company, you can also research employees in a company. For instance, if you look forward to working in a particular company, you can research the employee and find out how it feels like to work in that particular company.

d.   Keep your professional contact

How many contacts have you been able to keep and follow-up with from all the career fairs and conferences that you have attended over the years?

It may be a bit difficult for you to maintain contact and communication with all the contacts on the business cards that you have stuffed in your folder. With LinkedIn, staying connected is fast and easy, because you can send and receive messages and even share useful information.

e.   Get an opportunity to network

When it comes to accessing hidden jobs, networking is key. You don't have to worry if you don't have the opportunities to attend career conferences and workshops to network with people, LinkedIn has got you covered.

With LinkedIn, you can network with almost anyone without having to meet with them. By simply searching and sending them a message, you can build and grow your network.

Even if you are the most reserved introvert, LinkedIn can help you build relationships with people in your field and even help you connect with mutual connections.

5 Ways You can use LinkedIn to Get a Job

You can have a LinkedIn account and still not be able to use LinkedIn to get a job. Creating a LinkedIn account is not all there is to using LinkedIn to get a job, this is because you can have a LinkedIn account and still underutilize the features and flexibility that LinkedIn offers you.

The secret to using LinkedIn to get a job is having a well-optimized LinkedIn profile. Having a poorly optimized LinkedIn profile is like creating a bill-board and then storing it in your back yard. If your LinkedIn profile is poorly optimized, you may not get as much view as you would love to.

If you are confused about how you can use LinkedIn to search and get a job, then these 5 tips are all you need to become a champ.

1.   Create a strong LinkedIn profile

A great LinkedIn profile is important in optimizing your LinkedIn account. Your profile is essential because it is what your connections will get to see at the end of the day. Your LinkedIn profile should be strong enough to allow people to get to know you.

Since your LinkedIn profile is such a big deal, then you should make sure you follow these tips:

a.   Your profile must be complete: The more complete your profile is, the more attractive it will be. According to research, profiles that are complete tend to get more reach and visibility than profiles that are not complete. For your profile to be complete, it means that you need to have a background image, headshot photo, headline, summary, experience, education, skills, achievements, etc.

b. Your profile must show employers the value that you are willing to bring through achievements that are relevant to your field and industry.

c. You should note that your LinkedIn profile is not your CV and should not be treated as one. Don't make the mistake of copying your CV and pasting it on your LinkedIn profile.

d. You should know that your profile must be well-optimized to attract visitors. Recruiters and employers practically search LinkedIn for possible candidates, so a well-optimized profile will easily appear in search results.

e. Your profile should give recruiters and employers the opportunity to get a feel of your personality. Employers love to know their prospective employees to a great extent, asides from what they can see on the candidate's CV. A complete profile, engaging posts, etc., can make the employer have a better feel of who you are even before the interview. Always write your profile in the first-person point of view.

2.   Build a targeted LinkedIn Network

When it comes to building connections and networks on LinkedIn, people have different ideas about how they would want to network or connect based on their personality. While some people are open to connecting and networking with literally anyone at all, others prefer to network only with people that they know.

Connecting with anyone or networking with only people that you know both have their disadvantages:
a. If you connect with anyone regardless of who they are, there is a high chance that you may not be able to sustain the connections because your interests don't align.

b. On the other hand, if you connect with only people that you know, you may be shutting your door to great opportunities. If the essence of LinkedIn is to network, then connecting only with people that you know defeats the essence of "networking". To effectively network on LinkedIn, you have to build a targeted network. The big question is how do you build a targeted network? If you are new to LinkedIn, these tips will help you create a targeted network.

Connect with your former colleagues

When you are just building your LinkedIn profile, you can begin with connecting with your former colleagues (these consists of people that you have previously worked with). The importance of connecting with your former colleague is that it will be easy for you to get an endorsement from other people because a least they know you. Your former colleagues can stand as referrals for you to land your next job.

Connect with your field or industry peers

When building your LinkedIn profile, you should connect with people in the same field or industry just like you. When you connect with people that are in similar job field like you, it allows you to learn about industry trends and also opens you up to opportunities.

Connect with companies and industry experts

You can build your network on this third level, which is with top companies on your list and industry experts. Connecting with top companies on your list and industry experts will help you reach out to these companies and also learn more about these companies. Industry experts can also help you build your knowledge and also guide you in your career journey.

3. Engage with your connections on LinkedIn

One of the greatest ways to use LinkedIn to find a job is to engage with the connections that you have already made on LinkedIn. The essence of LinkedIn is not for you to gather thousands of connections just for the fun of it. The essence of connecting with someone is to eventually build a relationship with that person.

One way you can retain your connections on LinkedIn is to maintain engagement with your connections. You would likely be remembered by your connections if you have been engaging with them. Engaging with your connections shows that you are interested in them. Your engagement can cause you to be noticed by a recruiter that may likely want to hire you or even recommend you for a position.

"Out of sight they say, is out of mind". So, to ensure that you are remembered by others especially recruiters, you have to be seen. How can you engage with your connections? Engaging with your connections is not a difficult thing to do, but doing this can make a lot of difference:

- You can share an article or link to a video that will benefit your network.
- You can increase engagement with your connection by asking intelligent questions that will elicit great response.
- Like and comment on other people's comment.
- Congratulate someone on a new job or a promotion.
- Offer advice on a subject that most of your connections can relate to.
- Shout out to your connections.

4. Let people know that you are available for a position

If you are actively searching for a job, you can make that clear on your headline so that when someone views your profile, they will be able to know at once that you are open to a job offer. You can do this by adding it to your headline. You can add it to your headline like this; "A digital marketer seeking business in need..."

5. Get involved in LinkedIn professional groups

Professional groups on LinkedIn allow you to connect with people with the same interest like you. Since you share the same interest with people in this group, it means that it will be easy for you to relate with these people on a certain level.

Asides from interactions, a lot of information is usually shared in groups. Ideas like; in demand skills to acquire, job adverts are usually shared in groups too. This can be quite different from what you may see on your LinkedIn job board because of the personal feel that being in a group gives you.

LinkedIn is an amazing platform that helps job seekers to a large extent, but you can only enjoy the benefits when you put in conscious effort into making it work. Using LinkedIn to find a job doesn't just end with using LinkedIn features. Having a great profile, engaging with your network, and building your connection are not enough to actually land a job with LinkedIn most times.

Even if you can connect with thousands of people on LinkedIn, you may not be able to gain much from them until you are able to reach out and affect them on a personal level. Going out of LinkedIn can help you create a real connection with your network. You can skype, message or even call people that you have connected with.

3.11 HOW TO FIND A JOB USING A RECRUITMENT AGENCY

No doubt, landing the job of your dreams can be quite challenging, but collaborating with a recruitment agency can be the solution you have been looking for. You know why? I'll show you why.

You might have a good CV and a selling cover letter, but finding those companies that are willing to hire you and attracting an interview invite is still a hurdle you would have to overcome. Using recruitment agencies might sound a bit indirect, but they can make the job search process easy and fast.

Many people think that recruitment agencies only help candidates get contract positions; this is not true because recruitment agencies can help you find full-time opportunities regardless of the stage you are at in your career. If you can't wait to see how this is possible, then you are reading the right book.

Before we go into how you can find jobs using recruitment agencies, we must look at what a recruitment agency is all about and what they do.

What is a recruitment agency?

A recruitment agency is also known as an employment organization that matches employers with employees. Recruitment organizations help companies fill vacant positions while they help job seekers find jobs.

Why do recruitment agencies exist?

Recruitment agencies exist to help employers find the best possible candidates. They do this by taking charge of the whole recruitment process; from crafting a job description to finally getting job candidates on board.

Why do companies use recruitment agencies?
Many job seekers are somewhat scared of recruitment agencies because they feel like if a company has a vacant position, why can't the company go ahead and recruit candidates to fill the position instead of using the service of a recruitment agency? The truth is, many companies especially large companies don't have time to sort through thousands of CVs and go through the process of selecting the best candidate especially when they are hiring for lots of positions.

Asides from large companies, small companies also make use of the services of recruitment agencies to make sure they get the best possible candidate for their vacant positions. Most small companies don't have the right resources to hire the right candidates for their positions.

This is where recruitment agencies come in – When a company (small & large) gets in touch with a recruitment agency to help fill a vacant position, the recruitment agency will help the company find and finally get the best possible candidate for the position.

Do you see why recruitment agencies are important?

- Recruitment agencies help save lots of time and

effort by handling all the recruitment process and putting forward only top quality candidates suitable for the position.

- While recruitment agencies help companies save time, they also help job seekers land jobs by making sure their CVs are well optimized and also making sure they are well coached for the interview too.

In basic terms, the recruitment agency is the middle man between the job candidate and the employer.

Why should you use a recruitment agency to find a job?

Do you see why recruitment agencies are important?

- Recruitment agencies help save lots of time and effort by handling all the recruitment process and putting forward only top quality candidates suitable for the position.
- While recruitment agencies help companies save time, they also help job seekers land jobs by making sure their CVs are well optimized and also making sure they are well-coached for the interview too.

In basic terms, the recruitment agency is the middle man between the job candidate and the employer.

Why should you use a recruitment agency to find a job?

We have been talking about recruitment agencies and what they do and how they can help you land a job. It is common for many job seekers to ask; "why should I use a recruitment agency when I can find lots of jobs myself on the internet?"

It is true that you can find lots of job vacancies yourself online, but using the services of a recruitment agency sure has some advantages that you may not be open to when you decide to find the jobs yourself.

If you are confused about whether you should use a recruitment agency or not, then you are reading the right book. Are you ready to find out why a recruitment agency is a great option for you? Let's get started.

a. It is free

One of the benefits of using a recruitment agency is that you get a lot of advantages without paying a dime. The services that a recruitment agency will offer you are mostly free, this is because the company instead of you is the client, and you don't have to pay to be considered for a job interview.

b. You don't have to search for jobs yourself, they will do the searching for you

When you register to work with a recruitment agency, they will ask you about your skills and experiences and let you know if they have jobs that fit your interest. Some recruitment agencies have their websites that allows job seekers to search and find jobs themselves.

A recruitment agency increases your chances of landing a job because most of the jobs they advertise are not common jobs. Most recruitment agencies have direct contact with the employers advertising for vacant positions, so there is a probability that the competition will be significantly low.

c. Various Benefits

Recruitment agencies provide various benefits for job candidates. If a job candidate finally gets the job, many recruitment agencies provide a lot of benefit for the candidates like health insurances, retirement plans, etc.

d. You'll get expert guidance from a professional

When you register with a recruitment agency, most likely, you would be allocated a recruiter that knows so much about the field that you would love to go into. This recruiter will make sure he/she guides you into the job market that you are interested in.

The recruiter will give you all the information you need to

know, including the best jobs that fits you, what employers are looking for, and whether your experience and skills are great for the job.

e. Recruitment agencies have jobs that you may not find anywhere

The good thing about the recruitment agency is that it enables you to search and apply for jobs that are hidden. Applying for hidden jobs gives you a greater chance to land a job sooner than other candidates might. A recruitment agency gives you the opportunities to be one of the few candidates to apply for the hidden jobs, do you know why? Many companies choose recruitment agencies as their only method of getting new employees on board because they prefer to leave the job to the recruiter rather than doing it themselves. This is why you would likely find jobs that you have not seen advertised anywhere on recruitment agency's job board or career page.

Okay, we have given some amazing reason why using a recruitment agency may be the best option for you. If you are ready to give this a try, then let's look at how you can find a job using a recruitment agency.

How to find a job using a recruitment agency

a. Find a good recruitment agency

Using a good recruitment agency can make the process of landing a job a lot easy for you. It may not be very easy for you to find a good recruitment agency if you are new to job search.

You can search on google for recruitment agencies around you. When you create a list, take each name and then look out for reviews about these agencies (forums are a good place to search for reviews). Another way to find out how good a recruitment agency is, is by asking and getting direct endorsement from someone that has used their services.

b. Be serious

Many times, recruitment companies have some processes that they follow to get the best candidates for an open position. Sometimes, these processes can be long and tiring but you should take it seriously.

Processes like mock interviews and assessment test can seem like a waste of time especially when you know it is not the company that you are going to be working for that is interviewing you. Regardless of how tiring or rigorous the process might be; you must take it seriously.

It is necessary for you to be serious because the recruiter is not just after your skills and experience, your attitude to work also matters.

c. Be honest

Once you have been able to find a recruitment agency and have been allocated a recruiter, try as much as possible to be honest. The recruiter needs you to be honest about a lot things that can determine whether or not you will get the job you want. Be honest about what your career goals are, and clearly communicate this to the recruiter. The recruiter should know whether you are looking for a permanent position, flexible work from home job, or if you just want to acquire skills that will position you for better employment. You should also be open about what your employment situation has been like. The recruiter should know if you have a gap in your work history or if you have been job-hopping. Being honest with the recruiter will help the recruiter figure out how to explain these things better with the employer.

d. Keep an open mind

As much as you have career goals and the kind of jobs that you would love to do, it is also important for you to keep an open mind when you are working with a recruitment agency. Many times, a recruitment agency may have jobs that are not exactly what you are expecting.

Even if you can reject an offer that you feel doesn't suit you, it is also important you are open to offers that can prepare you for a better offer in the future. If you are an entry-level candidate, then it is really important for you to keep an open mind because you are just starting your career.

e. Keep in touch

Recruitment agencies deal with lots of candidates every time, so you should know that you are not the only person the recruiter has to respond to. Because the recruiter is helping other job candidates, it is good you follow-up with the recruiter to find out about your progress and to also find out if there are other positions that fit you. You can keep in touch by sending thank you mails after the interview, request for feedbacks after sending your CVs or after an interview, etc.

Things to consider before choosing a recruitment agency to get a job

- What kind of agency is it?
- What kind of jobs do they offer?
- Do they have job openings regularly?
- How effective are their services?
- How successful have they been over the years?
- What are other people saying about them?

Using a recruitment agency to find a job can make your job search process a lot easy, especially if you are using a good recruitment agency like MyJobMag and if you also understand what you are doing. Getting used to the process and selling yourself properly to the recruiter can make all the difference.

Note: You can make use of more than one recruiter to fast track your job search process. If you are new to job search, then it is good you start it right with MyJobMag's recruitment services.

3.12 CHAPTER SUMMARY

Congratulations! You now know how to search for and find jobs, if you have carefully read this chapter.

In this chapter, we concentrated on job search methods that work, which are: networking (a means to access hidden jobs), using social media (Great tool for researching and communicating with employers), using job boards (having access to millions of job listings).

Research shows that more than 80% of employers and recruiters search the internet to learn more about you before they consider employing you for a job. If an employer can't find you online, then you stand a risk of not getting qualified for the job.

When it comes to finding a job, it is good for you to be aware of trends and methods that work to be sure you are on the right track.y

CHAPTER 4

WRITING A CV

We are sure you must have heard about a CV many times, so what do you think a CV is? We would say a CV is your marketing tool, you know why?

It is simply because the CV is a promotion for a special product _ you!

Your CV gives you the first opportunity to present yourself as a great hire to your prospective employer, and hopefully, it will lead to an interview. This is the magic wand you need to call forth the all anticipated job interview.

You must have come across many articles online on how to write a CV, CV dos and don'ts, etc. While there is no single correct format for a CV, it is also important that every CV follows some rules. A good CV should express some interesting and unique things about you, like your skills, your experience that is related to the job that you are looking for, etc.

From your CV, a potential employer should be able to tell that you are the best person for the job looking at your skills, qualification, experience, and interest. Your CV should be able to motivate an employer to invite you for an interview to learn more about you.

Okay, we have almost introduced the CV too much, but what exactly is a CV?

4.1   What is a CV?

In simple terms, a CV is a detailed document that highlights your professional and academic history. A CV typically includes information like work experience, achievements, qualification, skills, etc. A CV is usually used to apply for a job.

Okay, now that you understand what a CV is, why then do you think you should write a CV? Well, why some people don't see the importance of writing a CV, many people see and understand the importance of writing a CV.

If you have been wondering why you should write a CV in the first place, then you should take a look at the next section.

4.2 IMPORTANCE OF WRITING A GOOD CV

Your CV should effectively present your values as a potential employee. You should also not forget to express your values in a few seconds, you know why? It is simply because recruiters spend only 6 seconds reading a CV. You may think that writing a good CV doesn't directly guarantee a job because you still have to be interviewed by the employer. Yes, a CV doesn't guarantee you a job, but at least it gets your foot in the door.

Since it is impossible for you to walk up to an interviewer to answer questions about yourself as regards the job that you are applying for, it is good you write a CV. A good CV can always stand on its own to answer any question that a recruiter might have. Asides from getting your foot in the door, a good CV is important for the following reasons:

a.   **It is your first contact with your potential employer**
Your CV is the first impression that your prospective employer will have about you. How would you love to appear on a date with someone you are meeting for the first time? It is only normal for you to make sure you get your general appearance right because you want to present yourself in a certain way to your date. The same thing happens with your CV. Your CV is the first impression you give your prospective employer in the selection process that will determine whether or not you will get the job. You know what they say about the first impression; your CV is your first impression.

b.   **It will help you thrive in the 21st century job market**

Many people believe that getting a job used to be easier in the old days. Yes, but gone are the days when getting a college or a university degree will get you a job on a platter.

Well, this doesn't work anymore considering the job market that we are in now. This is the 21st-century job market, and in this kind of job market, the competition is stiff.

Landing a job in today's job market means that you will be competing for a single position with a least 249 job seekers (according to Forbes Survey) that might even be more qualified than you are.

As the talent pool stretches, the job market stiffens more with the competition. One of the ways to increase your chances in this job market is to get your CV right. A good CV will put you in an advantaged position.

c.   **It helps to reduce job search frustrations**

Sending out a bad CV is a total waste of time, why? Because it will not get the attention you would love for it to get. Recruiters don't spend much time reading a CV, and if it is a bad one, it will be trashed in no time.

One of the most frustrating things about searching for a job is working hard to write a CV/applying to jobs and getting rejected every single time. This frustrating experience is what a bad CV can cause for you.

You may not directly be the cause of the rejection you have gotten from the 100 applications you sent out, it is most likely your CV (not up to par CV).

A good CV saves you time and effort; at least with a good CV, you are sure that your foot is on the right path. Sending out a bad CV is simply fighting a lost battle, so what sense does it make to start losing when you are fighting a competitive battle.

4.3 HOW TO WRITE A GOOD CV

Writing of a CV can be somewhat difficult, that is why we are presenting you 5 easy steps on how to write a professional CV for a job. The reason is that there is no one specific format for writing a CV and you will have to determine exactly the right CV for the position you are applying to.

You will always need to tailor your CV's content to the individual jobs you are applying for because one type of job might need you to emphasize a specific area whereas another might require you to elaborate on a different area.

One of the best ways to know what CV is right for your industry is to look at examples of what others have done. You can do this by either researching them online or by reaching out and talking to either your mentor or peers who are already employed.

Always remember though, that these examples are only examples and you should make sure your CV is specific to you and not just a copy of what someone else has done. You are unique and your CV should reflect that. With that being said, however, there are some common CV features you should keep in mind when writing yours.

4.4 WHAT TO INCLUDE ON YOUR CV

Even if your CV can be flexible to suite some information like your skill set, professional experience, interest etc. There is still some information that an employer would love to see on your CV regardless. You know that employers don't spend the whole day reading your CV. An average recruiter will spend 6 seconds to glance through your CV. Surprised right?

When employers read your CV, they are reading your CV to determine if you are the best person for the job. So to appeal to your prospective employer's judgement, you must figure out what your prospective employer wants to see at a glance.
If you are confused about what employers are looking for on your CV, then you don't have to worry because we've got you covered.

To create an outstanding CV, you have to include the following information:

Name, professional title and contact information

The first thing the recruiter should see when they open your CV should be your name, professional title, and personal contact. This information should be positioned at the top of your CV. Putting this information at the top of your CV gives the employer an idea of who you are at a glance.

Your name should be the title of your CV followed by your professional title. You should not use titles like; "Curriculum

Vitae", "CV" on your CV, you know why? It does not serve any purpose.

When it comes to adding your contact details to your CV, your email and phone numbers are important. A recruiter will likely call you on phone to inform you of the interview after they must have sent you an email to that effect.

You can decide to add your social media account in this section. Many employers search for candidates on social media to know more about them.

Gary Olusegun
Adminstrative Assistant
0804-7657-432
sample@gmail.com
3, Ike Street, Ikeja

(The example above shows the name, professional title, and contact information).

Personal Profile

Your profile is also known as your personal statement. Your personal statement is a piece of writing usually not more than 2 or 3 paragraphs that appears at the top of your CV that gives a summary of who you are, your skills, your achievement, experience, your career goals and finally; the reason for your application.

You can write an amazing CV, but not having a personal statement on your CV or having a poor one can make your CV not get the attention that it should get. A personal statement is what captivates the recruiter's attention to your CV.

It is good for you to tailor your personal statement to the job that you are applying for. Don't forget to keep your personal statement short and interesting and a few sentences long. To achieve this, you can build your personal statement around the following:

- Who you are

- What you do
- Why you are applying for the role

This example will help you write your personal statement

Personal statement example: *"A team player, with a commitment to customer service, who possesses a long track record of working in various administrative roles, coupled with good PC skills and the ability to communicate confidently at all levels.*
Apart from being immediately available, I have a strong background in general administration along with experience of working within a customer focused company like yours."
(Learn more about how to write a personal statement).

Job Experience and Employment History

This section allows you to list your previous jobs, work experience and internships. You must include this section in your CV because it gives the employer an idea of what you can do. Employers find it easier to hire a candidate that has functioned in a particular role, rather than someone that has little or no experience at all. That is why it is good for you to arrange your work experience in reverse chronological order so that the employer can see your most recent work experience first.

When you are listing your previous positions of employment, you should state your job title, the employer (company name), the dates that you worked, and a few sentences that summarize the role. Put your key responsibilities, skills, etc. in bullet points to aid readability.

MMM YYYY - MMM YYYY
Company Name, Location

    Position title

Outline

XXXXXXXXXXXXXXXXXXXXXXXXXXXXXXXXXXXXXXXXXXXXXXXX-

XXXXXXXXX

Key Responsibilities
XXXXXXXXXXXXXXXXXXXXXXXXXXXXXXXXXXXXXXXXXXX-
XXXXXXXXX

Key Achievement/ Projects

XXXXXXXXXXXXXXXXXXXXXXXXXXXXXXXXXXXXXXXXXXX-
XXXXXXXXX

Education and Qualification

Your education is another important section that should be included in your CV. Many job descriptions usually come with educational qualification/specification. Just like you listed your job experience, you should also list your educational qualification in reverse chronology. Include the name of the institution and the dates you were there, followed by the qualifications and grades that you achieved.
If you recently graduated from school, you can list a few of your relevant modules, assignments or projects underneath your educational qualification. If you have gone a little further along in your career journey and have many certifications, you can add that to your qualification.

You can write your educational qualifications this way:
Institution name - Dates (From - to)
Qualification/Subjects - Grade

Skills/Abilities

If you are writing a CV that is focused on showing your work experience, knowledge and expertise, then you are writing a functional CV. In this kind of CV, you arrange your job skills chronologically.

Asides from writing a functional CV, your skills are one of the most important information that you should include on your

CV. It is important to add skills that are relevant to the job you are applying for at a strategic section of your CV. You can study the job description carefully to understand what skills are most important to perform the job. Make sure you arrange your skills in order of relevance.

Interests and Abilities

Interest and abilities are very important aspects of your CV especially when you don't have enough work experience. If your CV is lacking work experience, your interest and abilities will provide a way for you to show your prospective employer that you can do the job.

- You should put the following into consideration when you are writing your interests and abilities:
- Add the abilities and interest relevant to the job
- Add your volunteering activities.
- Don't just write a list of your interests and abilities
- Make sure your interest show your commitment.
- Don't use the term "hobby" when you are talking about your interests and abilities because it does not sound professional.
- Avoid including activities that suggest that you are a loner. Employers look forward to hiring someone that can work well in a team. Avoid writing activities like reading unless it is related to the job.

4.5 WHAT NOT TO INCLUDE ON YOUR CV

Irrelevant work experience

Any work experience that is not related to the position you are applying for should not be added to your CV. As much as adding your work experience to your CV is important, it is also important you include only experiences that are related to the job that you are applying for.

Personal information

Personal information like; your marital status, religious preference etc. Any information that does not suggest that you are the best person for the job should not be added to your CV. Employers are not interested in knowing your personal details; they want to know if you are the best candidate for the position.

Your hobbies

Your prospective employer does not care about what you love to do in your spare time if it is not related to the job. There is no need including your hobbies to your CV if it is not related to the job.

Blatant lies

There is no point lying on your CV to please the recruiter. Lying does not make you qualified for the job. According to statistics, 75% of hiring managers can spot a lie on a CV. Lying about your skills and qualifications may even get you disqualified for the position.

A career objective

A career objective may not be necessary in your CV. If you have applied for the job, then your objective is clear (you want the job). You should write a personal statement instead to emphasize why you think you are the best candidate for the job.

Physical description

It is not necessary to add a physical description of yourself to your CV. Even if you think you have a great physical feature, it may not appear great to the recruiter. You should leave this information to the recruiter to discover during the interview.

Salary information

Compensation rate differs from company to company. Adding your salary information to your CV may have a negative effect on you more than you think. Putting your salary information can make you earn lesser than you should earn. It can also disqualify you from the position, as the information may suggest to the recruiter that you are not open to negotiation at all.

Reference

If the recruiter wants to talk to your referee, then they will let you know and ask you to provide that information. Writing "Reference upon request" may also be unnecessary. However, it is good you make plans for this beforehand to give you ample time to prepare.

4.6 CV FORMAT FOR FRESH GRADUATES (COMMON FEATURES OF A CV)

So what CV format works in recent times? We will address this by looking at the best features a good CV should have. Let's begin.

Start by first listing everything you can about your background information and then build out from there. To help you get started, here are a few of the most often seen sections of CVs that you might expect to include when writing your own.

1) Who are you?
A CV should always include your basic information starting with your name, address, telephone number, and email. Include a brief bio of yourself. Depending on the industry you are going into, a short blurb about who you are might be all you need to catch a recruiter's eye and get called in for an interview. If you do decide to include a brief bio, make sure it's well written and original.

2) What have you done?
As a CV is a thorough detailing of your history, that includes your educational history as well as your work experience and any training you might have received. When detailing your edu-

cational history, you want to do it in reverse chronological order. Be sure to include the full list of your degrees, including those you've already earned and any you might be currently pursuing as well as where you received your education.

Be sure to list the years of your graduation. If you are the author of a dissertation or thesis, you would include that information here as well as the name of your advisor.

For your work history, you want to include not only where you've worked, but also any applicable experiences related to that work. If you're an educator and you're not only teaching but also working in a research lab or facility, you would want to include that here. Field experience, leadership experience, related volunteer work and any other experience that relates to your employment goes in this section.

3) What do you like?

Unlike a resume, a CV often includes a section that covers your areas of interest. While this might seem unusual, it can provide a potential employer with a lot of insight into who you are, which is why it's so important to make sure you handle this section carefully.

While it might be tempting to just list your hobbies here and hope for the best, it's a good idea to expand on what you do in your free time as well as why you do it. Are you a soccer buff who loves to go to watch soccer? Rather than just listing "Soccer" on your CV, flesh it out a bit.

"As a lover of soccer, I enjoy spending my weekends immersed in a world where I coach a team of teenagers in my locality on everything soccer."

Do you have leadership skills outside of your work that you enjoy participating in? List those here as well.

This section is also a great place to list any interests that you have that relate directly to the job you're applying to. Are you working on obtaining employment as a culinary specialist? List your interest in food blogs and magazines.

No matter what you list here, try to include a range of interests that demonstrate who you are when you're not working at your job. Of course, try not to include information that would merely stuff things into your CV to give it length. It's perfectly fine to list your interests, but keep it within reason. List the things that are the most relevant to what you are looking for work-wise. It's not necessary to list every extracurricular activity you've ever participated in.

5) Skills
How many languages do you speak? Are you fluent in multiple tongues? What about computer programs? Are you an accomplished graphic designer who has extensive knowledge of a specific software? List that too!

6) Awards and recognitions
Have others recognized you for the work you've done? Do you have any awards or honours that you've received for teaching? How about for service or work? Have you applied for and received any grants or scholarships? Those go here! This is also where you want to include things like fellowships or patents.

7) Publications
Are you an author of any papers, articles or books? Are you an expert in your field and thus find yourself speaking at conferences, panels or symposiums? Make sure you list those and give a brief description of each so your reader knows what you've done and where.

8) Professional membership
Are you a member of any professional organizations, guilds or clubs? Make sure to include if you've held any offices or positions within those organizations and how long you've been with them.

9) Others

Other sections you might include in your CV (depending entirely on the job you're applying for) include:

- Study Abroad
- Exhibitions
- Professional Licenses and/or memberships
- Consulting Work
- Professional Development
- Research Experience
- Teaching Experience

Remember, your CV should be specific to the industry or area of work you're entering, so while much of the basic information should be fairly standard, always find examples that relate to the job you're after to ensure that you're including all the necessary things.

Formatting

You want to make sure that your CV is carefully and logically laid out and that it reads well. Yes, you're including a lot of information in this document, but don't try to cram everything in all at once.

- Organize it using topical headings and be considerate in how you lay it out and how you order it. While the order of topics in a CV is flexible, it's a good idea to keep in mind that what you list first will receive the most attention. Try to arrange your sections so that they highlight your strengths concerning the position you are applying to.
- Make sure your font is readable and that you are consistent with any formatting you decide to use.
- When you're working on a resume, it's common to use a type of formatting called "gapping." Gapping is when you take a full sentence and cut it down to the most basic components in to convey the most amount of information in the least amount of words.

- When writing your CV, you will want to use full sentences. It's also important to work with action words that will help to not only draw in the reader but keep them engaged in what they're reading.

Here, let us show you the difference. Let's pretend you were a Logistics Manager in a service department at a company. If you were writing a resume and utilizing gapping, you might note your experience like this:

Public Relations Manager (2008-2012)
Team Manager.
Responsible for customer service.

Again, this example is perfectly acceptable for a resume. For a CV, however, you want to make sure you're including more information and utilizing your action words.

Example:
I worked as a Public Relations Manager from 2008 to 2012. During that time, I oversaw and led a team of twenty employees committed to providing quality customer service.

Need another example?
Rather than saying you were just a marketing manager for five years (perfectly acceptable on a resume), make sure to include words that convey what you did.
Example:
"I spent five years refining my abilities as a negotiator and motivator, using my skills as a problem solver to help persuade clients to try new and exciting products"

- When printing your CV, always print your pages single-sided. Yes, it's longer than a resume, and it's tempting to try to save paper by printing double-sided, but resist that temptation!
- As a CV is longer than a resume and can often run into several pages, make sure you include page numbers on every page except for the first one.

Length: Your CV doesn't have to be super long for you to pass the information across to your employer. If you are applying for an entry-level job, then a one-page CV is just fine. If you are a professional, then a CV of 2 – 3 pages is not bad too.

Heading: It is good you introduce each section with a heading. It makes your CV clearer, and also helps the recruiter locate important information on your CV easily.

Font type and size: You will most likely send your CV to your prospective employer in digital format. So this means you have to choose your font size and colour carefully. Your font size should not be too big, so you don't look unserious. The font colour should be clear and sharp enough for the employer to read. Your CV should be between 10 – 12-point size, use font types like Calibri and Arial.

Page Margin: Margins make your document appear neat and easy to read. You should keep your margins around 2.5 cm; it should also not be less than 1.27 cm.

Proof-reading: Be consistent with your formatting to give your CV that clean and neat look.
Typos are little errors that can spoil all you have put in so much effort to do. To avoid this from happening, you should proof-read your CV to be sure there are no errors.
Grammarly can be a great proofreading tool for you.

Saving the file: Save your file in a format that can be easily accessed by the employer. Saving your CV in special format may make it difficult for someone that does not have the software to access the document. Save your CV as a PDF file to ensure recruiters can open it on any device. A PDF will also help you maintain formatting.

4.7 USING A CV TEMPLATE TO CREATE YOUR CV

CV templates are great because at least they help with the structure and format of your CV, you may need to fill in your information where necessary. While CV templates are great, they are no magic bullet that will allow you just plug and play, and then you magically get an interview invite.

Whether you are using a template or creating your CV from scratch, make sure your CV reflects you and it is also customized to the job that you are applying for.

CV templates indeed help you with the form and structure of your CV, but you would have to do somethings yourself, like:

1. Checking for typos.
2. Tailoring your CV to the role.
3. Tell the truth in your CV.
4. Change the name of the file, and give the file a unique name.
5. Proofread the document and check for grammatical errors.
6. Add your contact in the right place.
i. Full name
ii. Professional title
iii. Email address
iv. Telephone number
v. LinkedIn profile
vi. Home address

7. Start with your personal statement.

8. List your relevant work experience in the appropriate place on your CV.

9. Fill in your educational qualifications in the right places.

(See CV templates that you can use to create your own CV)

4.8 Frequently Asked Questions About Writing A CV.

When it comes to CV, we know that you would have many questions especially if you are writing one for the first time. To answer some of these questions, we have put together a list frequently asked CV questions from job seekers like you.
The answers to these CV FAQs will sure answer your questions too.

a. What is a CV?

Answer: CV (Curriculum Vitae) means a course of life in Latin. It is an in-depth document that can be laid out over two or more pages and it contains a high level of detail about your achievements, a great deal more than just a career biography.

b. What is a Resume?

Answer: A resume or résumé is a concise document typically not longer than one page as it is assumed that the reader will not dwell on your document for long. This includes your basic career information.

c. What is the difference between a CV and a Resume?

Answer: The main difference between a resume and a CV is that a CV is intended to be a full record of your career history and a resume is a brief, targeted list of skills and achievements.

d. When Should I use a CV or Resume for my Application?

Answer: Most employers will tell you what they want you to send in. However, it is advised that an experienced job seeker should use a CV for high profile job applications as this will show how much experience and expertise he has.

e. Are there any rules guiding CV and Resume writing?

There are no rules but be sure of the following:

- You do not tell a lie
- There are no typographic and grammatical errors

f. What should be included in my CV and Resume?

Bearing in mind, your objective for writing a CV or Resume, Your CV and Resume MUST include:

- Your Full name
- Contact information: Physical address, Phone number, email address
- Education
- Experience

g. Your CV and Resume may or may not include the following:

- Career Objective or Brand Statement
- Professional Certifications/Qualifications/Licenses
- Achievements/Publications
- Skills
- Hobbies/Interests
- Referees

h. Your CV and Resume should NOT include the following:

- Previous Salary
- Reason for leaving your previous job(s)
- Religion
- Race
- Date of Birth
- Health Information
- Phone number, email addresses or names of past employers.

These are not relevant to your job and should be discussed in person during an interview if they are a source of concern.

i. How do I ensure that my CV and Resume are attractive to employers?

Bearing in mind that a recruiter should be able to tell at a glance what you can offer, what your qualifications are and what experiences you have. We do recommend that you craft a brand statement and place it at the beginning of your CV/Resume.

Below is an example of a brand statement:
"With a Master's degree in Project and Construction Management and having worked as a Project Manager for 8 years in the oil and gas sector, I love to build formidable project teams from the scratch who can deliver top-notch projects on budget and within specified time frame"

j. What Resume format is best to use?

A chronological resume is the typical style most employers expect to see. The functional resume is popular with career changers, people with little work experience (like students and recent grads), or those who've been out of the work force for an extended leave. Mixed (combined format) resumes combine the chronological and functional formats. And a Curriculum Vitae (CV) is mainly for professors, teachers, lawyers, scientists and related professionals.

k. Can I access CV templates for free?

Yes, we have a couple of templates that you can download and use for FREE. You can access them on our website.

l. Can I get professional help in preparing my CV/Resume?

Yes, you can get help to prepare your CV and Resume. MyJobMag also offers a professional CV Writing Service that can help you get hired.

4.9 CV EXAMPLES

Writing a CV may not be a walk in the park especially if you are writing one for the first time. With everything that you have read about CV writing, writing a CV should not be a difficult thing for you to do. Well, if this is your first time you may need some form of guide to write a good CV.

These CV example will serve as a guide for you to write your CV.

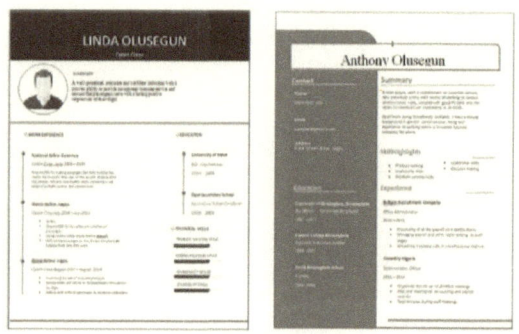

Figure 4.9.0 *CV Examples. (Adapted from MyJobMag CV templates).*

I am sure you must have been trying your hands on CV writing, especially after reading this chapter. If you have been trying out CV writing, then it would necessary for you to assess the CV you have written to be sure it is good enough before you start sending it out.

Assessment Exercise

We have discussed CV writing extensively in this chapter, so for this exercise, you are simply going to fill out the checklist to ensure you create a good CV. There are several questions under every section, all you have to do is to indicate 'Yes' or 'No' against the different questions.

Your response to the different questions will give you an idea about your areas of strengths and the areas you need to pay more attention to on your CV.

First Glance	Answer	
Question	Yes	No
Does you CV look original?	☐	☐
Is your CV attractive enough to take a recruiter's 6 seconds?	☐	☐
Did you include a personal statement?	☐	☐
How visually appealing is your CV?	☐	☐
CV Sections	Answer	
Question	Yes	No
Are all the sections represented on your CV?	☐	☐
Are the sections of your CV in the right place?	☐	☐
Are you leaving out an important information in your sections?	☐	☐
Accomplishments	Answer	
Question	Yes	No
Did you list your accomplishments in your CV?	☐	☐
Are you measuring your accomplishments well?	☐	☐
Does your accomplishment begin with active verbs?	☐	☐
Career Goals	Answer	
Question	Yes	No
Is my CV a one size fits all CV?	☐	☐
Is my CV targeted towards my career goal?	☐	☐
Is your career goal relevant to the position you are applying for?	☐	☐
How clear is the structure of your career goals?	☐	☐
Usefulness	Answer	
Question	Yes	No
Is the information on your CV what hiring managers want to see?	☐	☐
Does your CV support your personal statement?	☐	☐
Did you include keywords that are relevant to the job that you are applying?	☐	☐
CV Style	Answer	
Question	Yes	No
Is your CV written in the first person narrative?	☐	☐
Have you made sure there are no typos on your CV?	☐	☐
Are the lists on your CV written in reverse chronology?	☐	☐

Figure 4.9.1 *CV assessment exercise. Use the table above to assess your CV.*

4.9.1 CHAPTER SUMMARY

Congratulations! You have come a long way and you are almost done. We are glad that you now know how to write a CV, are you not happy with yourself too?

You know that a CV is a really important tool when it comes to job search, and it is fulfilling to know that writing a CV is no longer a big deal to you. This chapter aims to expose you to CV writing, and also to help you learn how to write a CV that can help you land the job of your dreams.

If you carefully read this chapter, you will notice that we extensively talked about the CV and everything that relates to CV writing. We made sure we extensively talked about CV writing because we understand how important it is to you, and we are happy you are good to go now.

CHAPTER 5

WRITING A COVER LETTER (WINNING THE JOB SEARCH WITH YOUR COVER LETTER)

You have spent some generous amount of time studying this book from chapter 1, and we sincerely congratulate you. You have learned how to find jobs both online and offline, how to network, and how to write a CV. Yes, you have done a great job, but there are a few things you still need to do to ensure you land the job of your dreams.

It could be tempting for you to think this way: I now know how to find jobs and I have a great CV, so do I need a cover letter? Yes, you do. Your cover letter can be the thing that will trigger a recruiter's interest in your CV which can lead to an interview invite and to a large extent prevent your CV from being ignored. You see why it's good for you to put in the effort to write a good cover letter.

In this chapter, we are going to be discussing the cover letter in details. The essence of this chapter is to help you have a good grasp of all you need to know about the cover letter as your job search tool.

Before we go into all the details, you must understand what a cover letter is and how important it is to help you land your dream job.

5.1 WHAT IS A COVER LETTER?

A cover letter is a document that provides extra information about your skills and experience which is mostly accompanied by a resume.

A well-written cover letter gives more information than what is on your CV, and it goes ahead to elaborate on this information for the recruiter, walking the recruiter through some of your great life and career achievements.

In very clear terms; a cover letter provides details about why you are qualified for a particular job. Your cover letter is more like a sales pitch about yourself and career that will help you get an interview invite.

Now you know you need to write a cover letter, but do you know why? You should not write a cover letter just because you know it is important, you should rather write a cover letter for tangible reasons.

5.2 10 REASONS WHY YOU NEED A COVER LETTER

If you don't see any reason why you should write a cover letter, then maybe you are yet to give it a deeper thought. A cover letter is important for many reasons, but we are just going to focus on these 10:

- It tells the employer who you are and why they need you.
- It allows you to highlight your strength.
- It shows that you are serious about the opportunity.
- It complements your CV.
- It sets up the need for a follow-up.
- It paves the way for a job interview which might hopefully lead to a job offer.
- It will explain in detailed terms the values that you will bring to the job.
- It will allow you to add extra information that you may not be able to add to your CV like; where you saw the job vacancy, reasons for employment gaps, etc.
- A cover letter allows you to direct your application to a particular person.
- A cover letter allows you to talk about the position that you are applying for, and also why you think you are the best person for the job.

Okay, you know why you should write a cover letter now, so

what next. Well, you need to know what makes up a cover letter. We are going to be looking at cover letter elements in the next section.

5.3 ELEMENTS OF A COVER LETTER

Your cover letter could just be that little difference between getting selected for a job interview and missing out on the job of your dreams. This is true even if it looks like job boards have changed the way people apply for jobs because most times all you need to do is to fill in your details in the application boxes and spaces. Regardless of how the internet has made job application look, many employers still demand cover letters.

Whether or not an employer asks you to send in your cover letter, it is important that you create a good cover letter that will make the best first impression by meeting the following criteria:

Formatting

A cover letter is a business letter and it should be treated as one. Every business letter has a format, so it is good for you to format your cover letter rightly. Your cover letter should be formatted with your address in the top right or left corner and the company's address in the opposite direction. Your address should be a few sentences long, then there should be an introduction.

Cover letter formatting still comes in place even when you are sending your application. It is good for you to save and attach your cover letter in a PDF file to maintain formatting. Following the guidelines will ensure that your visual copy is correct.

Recipient

Normally, your cover letter should be addressed to the particular person doing the hiring. It is important you take time to research the company so that you can identify the recruiter; it also shows the employer that you are interested in the job. Addressing your cover letter to the recruiter makes you stand out from other candidates. This is because while other candidates are writing a generic letter, you are being specific and intentional about the job.

Talking about addressing your letter to a particular recipient, how do you find out whom to address your letter to? Well, this is simple. You can check the company website for contact information; check LinkedIn for the company and employees. You can also ask a friend who works for the same company.

A Good Introduction

Many times, when people are asked to write about themselves they often start with; "My name is ...". This is not always wrong, but when you are writing a cover letter, your introduction should be more precise and related to the job and what you do. You should keep in mind that your introduction is like a hook or a clickbait. If your introduction does not give the recruiter an idea that you are the best person for the job, then you can say to a large extent that your introduction has failed.

Recruiters don't spend time reading a CV or a cover letter unless you give them a reason to. So, does your introduction give the recruiter a reason to read your cover letter?

Let's take some examples to make it even clearer. Let's compare introduction A and introduction B

Introduction A: *"My name is Samuel Peters and I am applying for the customer service position that was advertised on your company's website."*

Introduction B: *"With 5 years of customer service experience under*

*my belt, I believe that I have the skills required to excel in this posi-
tion..."*

Looking at these examples, what do you think?

Introduction A sounds boring and cliché, while introduction
B sounds precise, direct and engaging. Reading **introduction B**,
every recruiter will want to find out what makes the candidate
believe that he/she is capable of doing the job.

A Sales Pitch

Yes! We said it, a sales pitch. Your cover letter is a sales pitch
whether you like it or not and you should not see it as a mere
introduction of your CV. The earlier you start seeing your cover
letter as a sales pitch, the more intentional you will be when
writing your cover letter. Your cover letter is nothing different
from a sales pitch. The only difference is that you are talking
about how you are going to help the company.

The other parts of your letter should give some specific examples of your experience from your previous jobs, and the
skills you used to perform your duties. While looking at your
cover letter as a sales pitch, don't forget to focus on the benefit
that you bring to the company.

Your Knowledge of the Company

Recruiters want to hire someone that has some knowledge
about the company. It is only normal for an employer or a
recruiter to perceive that you are interested in the company
based on the amount of information that you have about the
company. It is only normal for you to know more about something that you are interested in.

One way that you can show the recruiter that you are interested
in the company is to display the amount of knowledge that you
have about the company. It is good that you show the employer
that you are specifically interested in the company and not just

applying for a job that you think you are a perfect fit for.

For example, if you are applying for a marketing position, you can research the company sales numbers and describe how your previous experience would help you take the company's sales to the next level. Recruiters' are usually impressed with this kind of details.

A call to action

What is a call to action? Just as the name implies; a call to action is a statement that will cause the reader to take the desired action. So what does it have to do with writing your cover letter? Remember that we said that your cover letter is like a sales pitch, and in a typical sales pitch; you would ask the reader to buy a product, subscribe to a newsletter, etc. well in a cover letter you are asking the recruiter to contact you for an interview.

Be careful to sound in a manner that will make the recruiter take your desired action. Instead of ending like this: *"Looking forward to hearing from you..."*. You should rather close your cover letter with this kind of call to action: *"...I am excited to meet and discuss how I can help this company..."*. This little difference can be the tiny reason why the recruiter will schedule an interview because he wants to know how you want to help the company grow.

Great Spelling and Good Grammar

Does good spelling and grammar matter? Yes, they do. Your cover letter could be the recruiter's first chance to have a glimpse of your personality before deciding if you will be a great fit for the role and position.

Bad spelling and poor grammar can affect the way a recruiter will perceive you without even being aware of it. A great eye for details is one skill that recruiters look forward to seeing in potential employees. Making noticeable mistakes with your spellings and grammar will go a long way to suggest to the recruiter that you are careless.

To prevent this from happening, always read your cover letter out slowly to make sure you take note of every error. You can give your cover letter to someone else to read for you to be sure you are not reading the content from your head.

Infuse Keywords into Your Cover Letter

Many times, recruiters and hiring managers scan through cover letters and CVs rather than taking out time to read them. Annoying right? But you can't do anything asides from finding a way to work around it. Infusing keywords related to the job helps your CV stand out from the crowd and also helps you make the recruiter see that you fit into their specification.

Keywords are specific little words that employers may be looking out for when they read a CV or cover letter. You will often find these keywords in the job description, requirement or qualification section of the job vacancy. It is good you take some of these keywords and infuse them into your cover letter to make it stand out from every other one. For example; if the recruiter is looking for someone with Graphic Design experience, you should mention your specific experience using the Adobe suite instead of generally saying that you are familiar with graphic design.

Uniqueness

Your cover letter should stand out. When we say your cover letter should stand out, we don't just mean that it should stand out from that of others. We mean that it should also stand out from your CV. Your cover letter is what will create an interest in the mind of your recruiter for them to look forward to reading your CV. However, your cover letter should not be another form of your CV. It should not be a summary of your CV. Your cover letter should be more like a preview that an employer gets to see. Something that will drive their interest in your CV, just like a movie preview will do. Don't make the mistake of summarizing your CV to form your cover letter. The truth is they work together, but they also perform different functions.

Writing a cover letter may not be an easy thing to do especially if you are writing one for the first time. These elements will sure give you a heads way to write a great cover letter if you carefully go through it.

5.4 A GUIDE TO WRITING A PERFECT COVER LETTER

It is good that you now understand the elements that make up a cover letter. Since you know that now, it is time for you to see how you can put it into practice by seeing how these elements will form a cover letter.

So, this guide will lead you on the different steps that will lead up to writing a cover letter eventually. Ready! Let's jump right into it.

A good cover letter should have a heading which usually appears at the beginning of the cover letter. The heading of your cover letter may vary depending on how you wish to send it.

If you are pasting it in the body of the mail, the format for the heading is slightly different from when you are sending it as a hard copy or an attachment. When you are pasting the cover letter in the body of the mail, you would need to use a strong subject line that will give the hiring manager the first impression about you.

If you are sending the hard copy of your cover letter, then your heading can be in this form:

Your Contact Information;

Your Name
Your Address
Your City, State Zip Code
Your Phone Number
Your Email Address
Date

Employer Contact Information;

Name
Title
Company
Address
City, State Zip Code

Write an Attention-Getting Introduction (First Paragraph)

The first paragraph of a cover letter is one of the most important aspects of the cover letter because that is what the recruiter or hiring manager will see first. To write a good cover letter, you should start your introduction with a greeting/salutation. You should start your cover letter salutation with *"Dear Sir/Madam/Mr./Mrs.,"*

You should be very careful not to address your hiring manager wrongly when you are trying to greet. You should take your time to research the hiring manager to find out his/her name, but if you can't do that, then you can simply address them as *"Dear Hiring Manager"*.

Another information you should add to your first paragraph is an introduction of yourself. After greeting the recruiter, you can then go ahead to introduce yourself. Introducing yourself doesn't mean you should tell the recruiter about your life history, you should rather introduce yourself by telling the recruiter the position you applied for and how you learned about the position. Always remember to keep your introduction short and straight to the point.

Sell Yourself to the Recruiter (Second Paragraph)

Since the cover letter is a marketing tool, then you should seize that opportunity to sell yourself to the recruiter/prospective employer. The second paragraph should more or less be a response to the job requirement, which allows you the opportunity to convince the hiring manager that you are a good fit for the position.

To properly sell yourself to your hiring manager or prospective employer, you should tell the hiring manager how your skills, previous experiences, and abilities will enable you to meet the company's expectations. Using words or phrases from the job advert in your cover letter can help you sell yourself better.

See Yourself in the Company (Third Paragraph)

In the third paragraph, you have to go a step above selling your skills and abilities to the hiring manager. This paragraph has to do with you being a part of the company's vision. The purpose of this paragraph is to make the hiring manager see how well you fit into the company. This paragraph will require you to research about the company and its vision. It will help explain how you fit into the company structure and how you can help push the company forward to achieve its goals.

Anticipate the Interview (Closing Paragraph)

In the closing paragraph of your cover letter, you should restate in a way the skills that make you a good fit for the job and why you would love to work for that particular company. You should also state that you would appreciate the opportunity of interview/employment discussions. Anticipating the interview will help you prepare better for the interview.

It is also important for you to explain what you intend to do to follow up and how you intend to do it (you can tell them that you would send them a mail in one week if you don't hear from them. Always remember to thank the employer for considering to read your letter.

For email cover letter, the closing can be quite different. You are expected to formally sign off when writing an email cover letter. The sign off can include your contact information or your email signature after your valediction.

Example:

Sincerely,
Rose Samuel
Data Entry Manager
Facebook/LinkedIn handle (if necessary)
001-005-6676 (telephone number)

5.5 HOW TO STRUCTURE AND FORMAT YOUR COVER LETTER

Have you thought of structures or formats you should use in your cover letter? Maybe not, but they are really important. Asides from the actual content on the page, the overall structure and format of your cover letter gives an impression of you to the hiring manager.

You should also structure and format your cover letter in such a way that it won't be sifted out on the ATS (applicant tracking system). Since some companies use the ATS to sift cover letters, then it is important for you to format your cover letter. Since ATS usually work based on keywords, then having the right keywords on your cover letter is key.

General Cover Letter Structure and Format

These are a few tips to help you format and structure your cover letter:

Fonts
When you are choosing a font for your cover letter ensure to keep it professional and simple. It is not advisable for you to use extremely fanciful fonts for your cover letter. It is better to stick with simple and professional fonts like Arial, Calibri, Ver-

dana, Times New Roman etc. Using fanciful font may not make your words clear enough to the recruiter or the ATS. You should also use size 10 – 12 points for easy/better readability. Using a bigger font size will make your letters look unprofessional and a smaller size may be difficult to read.

Alignment

The alignment of margin should be uniform throughout your document. You can use "11.5" margins, they are always safe. Using the proper margin prevents you from having a cramped up content. Then on alignment, it is advisable to align your content to the left.

Align your text left and use standard 1-inch margins all the way around. If your letter is spilling off onto a second page, first re-read it and see if there's anything you can cut. If you can't cut anything, you can consider shrinking the margins to ¾" or ½", but avoid going smaller than that so your cover letter doesn't look squished on the page.

Spacing

Good spacing is essential for the readability of your cover letter. Spacing your cover letter well will help the hiring manager read it easily. Make your cover letter single-spaced, it is good to add a space between each section of your cover letter.

Length

You should not have more than 3-4 paragraphs on your cover letter. Try to keep your cover letter on a single page. To achieve this, you must make sure you can communicate the essential information in fewer words.

File Format

Your cover letter should be saved in a compatible file format; the file formats should be one that can be easily downloadable. Sometimes, hiring managers use the Applicant Tracking System to sift cover letters, so it is necessary to save your documents in a compatible format (either MS word or PDF). You should take note of the name you give to your document; you can rename them to suit you. You can use this format of first name - last name - cover letter (e.g. John – Peters – cover letter.doc) to make it easily recognizable.

Edit and Proofread Your Cover Letter

It is very important to proofread your cover letter to be sure there are no errors before you attempt to send them out. It may sound small, but small errors can ruin the whole cover letter. You can read it over and over again or ask a friend to help you go through to make sure there are no errors. To make the editing and proofreading easier, you can make use of *Grammarly*; it is easier and faster.

5.6 THE DIFFERENT TYPES OF COVER LETTERS YOU NEED TO KNOW

A cover letter as the name implies, is a cover of your resume and not a duplicate. The cover letter is an introduction of who you are in relation to the position advertised. The cover letter type you wish to write largely depends on your reason and the purpose of the letter. The following are the types of cover letters you may wish to write:

The application cover letter

The application cover letter is usually written in response to a job opening that has been advertised. This type of cover letter should be formatted in a professional way to include a proper salutation and closing. When writing this kind of cover letters, you should make sure you give a detailed information about you and the company you are applying to. The information you give about yourself in this kind of cover letter should be one that shows why you are the best hire for the position advertised. The purpose of this letter is to sell yourself to your prospective employer.

Prospecting Letter/Letter of interest

A prospecting letter/letter of interest is a letter that is sent to inquire about any position that you may be qualified to fill. Sometimes, you may be aware that a company is recruiting, but you may not know the exact position they are recruiting for. The prospecting letter allows the employer know that you are interested in the company. This letter shows the skills in areas of work that you are interested in. You may also send your resume alongside this letter for future considerations.

Networking Letters

This kind of letter recommends you to a company you wish to work for based on the experience you have with other companies you have worked with. The networking letter can be written by another person on your behalf to recommend you for a position. This type of cover letter is very effective because it gives you the opportunity to add recommendations from people that you have worked with before. This kind of letters help you connect with people that may end up becoming your collaborators.

Direct Mailing

This type of cover letter is addressed to a particular person that may be your boss or the human resource manager. This kind of letter is written when you notice a particular company you want to work for and you decide to send a direct mail addressing someone in the company. The essence of this kind of cover letter is not necessarily to request for a job, but to build a relationship with the employer and to show your interest in the job. This is also a kind of cover letter that you can write to provide a solution. Some companies suffer serious bad economic times due to various reasons like; poor employee performance, poor revenue generation, over staffing etc. You can write a cover letter that tells the employers about how your skills will solve the situation of the company.

5.7 TOP COVER LETTER DOS AND DON'TS YOU SHOULD KNOW

A cover letter as the name implies is a cover of your resume and not a duplicate. The cover letter is an introduction of who you are in relation to the position advertised. The cover letter type you wish to write largely depends on the purpose of the letter. The following are the types of cover letters you may wish to write:

The application cover letter
The application cover letter is usually written in response to a job opening that has been advertised. This type of cover letter should be formatted in a professional way to include a proper salutation and closing. When writing this kind of cover letters, you should make sure you give detailed information about you and the company you are applying to. The information you give about yourself in this kind of cover letter should be one that shows why you are the best hire for the position advertised. The purpose of this letter is to sell yourself to your prospective employer.

Prospecting Letter/Letter of interest
A prospecting letter/letter of interest is a letter that is sent to

inquire about any position that you may be qualified to fill. Sometimes, you may be aware that a company is recruiting, but you may not know the exact position they are recruiting for. The prospecting letter allows the employer to know that you are interested in the company. This letter shows the skills in areas of work that you are interested in. You may also send your resume alongside this letter for future considerations.

Networking Letters
This kind of letter recommends you to a company you wish to work for based on the experience you have with other companies you have worked with. The networking letter can be written by another person on your behalf to recommend you for a position. This type of cover letter is very effective because it gives you the opportunity to add recommendations from people that you have worked with before. This kind of letters helps you connect with people that may end up becoming your collaborators.

Direct Mailing
This type of cover letter is addressed to a particular person that may be the boss or the human resource manager. This kind of letter is written when you notice a particular company you want to work for and you decide to send a direct mail addressing someone in the company. The essence of this kind of cover letter is not to request for a job, but to build a relationship with the employer and to show your interest in the job. This is also a kind of cover letter that you can write to provide a solution. Some companies suffer serious bad economic times due to various reasons like; poor employee performance, poor revenue generation, over staffing etc. You can write a cover letter that tells employers about how your skills will solve the problems of the company.

5.8 COVER LETTER EXAMPLES TO HELP YOU CREATE YOUR OWN

Writing a cover letter may not be easy especially if you are writing one for the first time. If you have been reading this book carefully, then you must have learned some cover letter writing tips. Well, there is no problem if you are writing a cover letter for the first time and feel like you need some form of guidance on how to go about it. Since it is always easy to do something working with a sample, we thought it is good for you to see a cover letter sample that will help you create your own.

Figure 5.8.0 *Cover letter examples. Use the cover letter examples to create your own.*

These cover letter examples will definitely give you a heads up as to how to go about writing your cover letter. Hope you will find it helpful.

We have almost come to the end of this chapter, but we can't wrap it up without carrying you along or putting you in charge of your work. So it's time for you to do a little assessment to see how well you are going about writing your cover letter. This assessment is more like a checklist that will help you ensure you are on the right track to creating a powerful cover letter.

All you have to do is; give answers to the following questions below:

General Information/Appearance of the Cover Letter	Answer	
Question	Yes	No
Do you have the same full contact information like the one you have on your CV?	☐	☐
Does your cover letter and CV match in style and format?	☐	☐
Does your Cover letter follow the standard format of: salutation, opening, body, and closing?	☐	☐
Is your cover letter longer than one page?		
Have you signed your name boldly and confidently?		
Cover Letter Writing Technique	Answer	
Question	Yes	No
Is your spelling and grammar good enough?		
Does your cover letter state the reason why you are writing a cover letter in the first place?	☐	☐
Did you include action verbs in your cover letter?	☐	☐
Is your cover letter concise and straight to the point?	☐	☐
Is your cover letter free of clichés that doesn't tell much about you specifically?	☐	☐
General Call-To-Action	Answer	
Question	Yes	No
Is your cover letter captivating enough to make the recruiter want to know more about you?	☐	☐
Does your cover letter prove to the employer that you are the right person for the job before they see your CV?	☐	☐
Building the Value of Your Cover Letter	Answer	
Question	Yes	No
Have you given examples of accomplishments that demonstrate your skills?	☐	☐
Have you demonstrated that you have a good knowledge of the company you want to work for?	☐	☐
Is your career goal relevant to the position you are applying for?		
Avoiding Cover Letter Mistakes	Answer	
Question	Yes	No
Have you told the employer what you can do for the organization rather than what they can do for you?	☐	☐
Have you requested for a call to action?	☐	☐
Have you avoided re-phrasing your CV?	☐	☐
Have you done enough research about the company?	☐	☐
Are you being too formal or too casual?	☐	☐
Is the information on your cover letter generic rather than specific to you?	☐	☐
Are you giving too much information?	☐	☐

Figure 5.8.1 *Cover letter assessment. Use the table above to assess your cover letter.*

5.9 CHAPTER SUMMARY

Wow! You are almost done with the book; you have just a few chapters left. Well, before you continue, it is good we congratulate you on your progress so far. Congratulations, you have actually done well.

Now, you have almost gotten all your job search tools right and we are happy you have. The aim of this chapter is to help you understand the rubrics of cover letter writing and how you can customize your own.

If you have carefully gone through this chapter, then, there is no doubt that you can write a good cover letter now. In the subsequent chapters, we will be talking about some other things you need to know about job search and even tips to help you cope with a new job.

CHAPTER 6

PREPARING FOR YOUR INTERVIEW
(WINING AT THE INTERVIEW)

Getting to the interview stage of the job search journey to a large extent feels like the journey is almost won. While this may be true, you should know that the journey is not yet won until the journey is won. It could be really exciting to realize that your commitment and hard work has finally paid off.

Getting an interview invite could seem like a mark of achievement for all the hard work you have put into examining yourself, writing a CV, writing a cover letter, and searching for jobs that best fits you. Well, while you have put in a lot already, this is not a good time for you to relax. You know why? This is simply because you are much closer to landing a job than you were before, and failing now will frustrate all the effort you have put into making your job search journey a successful one. It could be tempting for you to feel like you have gotten to the end of your job search journey when you get an interview invite.

Indeed your CV and cover letter allow you to impress your employer and it is also a chance for you to emphasize that you are the best person for the position that you are applying for. The moment an employer invites you for an interview, the recruiter views you as an employable candidate and would love to meet you in person to discuss your qualifications.

Now, you know that the recruiter sees you as employable, so what do you do about this?

The smart thing for you to do is to maintain the positive outlook that you have been able to create with your CV and cover letter. In preparation for your interview, your job is to express who you are and what you have to offer and also find out if the company is one that you can thrive in.

Passing your job interview is like putting that final seal on the deal. If you have never gotten an interview invite before, then meeting in person with the organization of your dreams may be discomforting, but you don't have to worry.

In this chapter, you will learn everything you need to know about the job interview process and how you can successfully pass and land the job of your dreams.

6.1 WHAT IS A JOB INTERVIEW ALL ABOUT?

Okay, we have been talking about a job interview from the introduction of this chapter, but what is a job interview all about?

The job interview is like every other form of an interview that involves a conversation between two parties to get to learn more about each other. The major difference between the job interview and every other kind of interview is that it involves an employer/recruiter and a job candidate.

A job interview is a conversation between a job applicant and an employer/recruiter/representative which is conducted to assess whether the job applicant should be hired. Employers usually make use of the interview as a part of their selection process.

Even though it is the employer that schedules an interview to learn more about a job candidate and to also decide if a particular candidate will be a great fit for the organization, the job interview is also a time for a job candidate to decide if an organization will bring out the best in them.

The job interview is an opportunity for an employer to meet with a job candidate and have conversations regarding the job.

6.2 WHY EMPLOYERS CONDUCT JOB INTERVIEWS

Just like we said earlier, conducting an interview is a major step that employers take in hiring an employee. The job interview is an opportunity for the employer to get information from job candidates asides from what is on the candidate's CV and cover letter.

Many times, job seekers often misunderstand the essence of a job interview. Job candidates think that an interview is a time for them to chitchat with the recruiter; employers don't conduct interviews to chat with you for the sake of it.

Employers conduct interviews for the following reasons:

a. To establish a rapport with the candidate

An employer may conduct an interview to create a form of rapport between himself and the job candidate. The interview allows the employer to meet with the job candidate in person. This is because the employer has known all he knows about the job candidate on paper.

So the interview allows the employer to validate the information that he must have seen on the CV and cover letter. Employers don't establish rapport with job candidates during an interview for the sake of it, they often do this to know the candidate more.

b. Gather information

Employers conduct interviews to gather information from the job candidate. Most times, before the interview, the employer must have noted down some things that he/she will love to find out from the job seeker. Sometimes, employers' pin-point specific details from a candidate's CV and uses the interview as an opportunity to validate some of those details. Employers use open-ended questions (how, what, when, etc.) to gather information about the job candidate.

c. To evaluate and compare job candidates

Employers often use the interview to check if a job candidate will be a great fit for the position that the organization wants to fill. Employers usually have a list of what they look forward to seeing in a prospective job candidate. Employers use the interview to rate a job candidate's performance, so that they can compare the performances of different job candidates. This will eventually help them with the hiring and selection process. Employers always take down notes when they interview every candidate as this helps them to remember key details for each job candidate.

d. To sell the company/organization

Just as you would love to land the job of your dreams, employers also look forward to hiring the candidate of their dreams. As job candidates try to sell themselves to an organization through their CVs and cover letter, employers also try to sell their company through the interview to prospective employees. When an employer sees a potential job candidate, because the employer wants the job candidate, the employer will most likely conduct an interview to kind of assure the candidate that the organization is a good organization to work for.

Just like employers conduct interviews for different reasons, every smart job seeker also honours an interview invite for some reasons, even if the ultimate reason why a job seeker will attend a job interview is to prove to the recruiter that they are best person for the job and probably land the job of their dreams.

Job seekers attend job interviews for the following reasons:

a. To learn more about the position

Many times, job seekers go for an interview to learn more about the position to determine if it is a job they can do. No job candidate will love to take up a job only to find out after a while that what they expected to see when they saw the job description is different from the actual job.

Even if you have an experience in the role that you are applying for, it is also good you know that no job is the same in every organization. This is why it is important for you as a job seeker to understand the specifics of a position with regards to a particular company.

b. To learn more about the organization

When it comes to getting a job, salary is not the only thing you should consider when it comes to deciding if you would accept a particular job offer. Although, it is important for you to know the salary that would satisfy you, but finding out about the company culture is also important too.

It is possible to get a good-paying job with a company that has a bad work environment. So, a job seeker should attend a job interview to find out how well they can thrive in that work environment.

Now, that you have discovered why job seekers attend job interviews, you must know how job seekers achieve their aims and goals.

The big question here is; how do job seekers achieve their goals through the interview process?

The truth is that no matter what a job seeker looks forward to achieving from the interview, which ultimately leads to landing a job, the only way you can achieve your goal from an interview is to prepare for the interview. Preparing for the interview will help you gain clarity on what you look forward to achieving. This includes knowing the questions that an employer will likely ask you during the interview and the questions you should ask to achieve your goals. In the next section, we are going to be looking at how you can prepare for your interviews.

6.3 HOW TO PREPARE FOR A JOB INTERVIEW

Researching the company/organization

You must have heard a lot of advice about researching the company/organization before going for an interview, and now we are advising you to do the same thing again. Now that you know the importance of researching the company/organization, the question again is how can you research a company/organization?

a. Visit the company's website

To research a company, you can start by visiting the company's website. Visiting the company's website will help you review the organization's mission, products, services and information about the company's culture. You can check the company's "About us" page to find out about the company's culture. It is also good for you to go through the entire website and read through some of the blog posts on the website to know more about the company.

b. Browse the company's social media handles

Once you have checked the company's website, the next thing you can do is to browse the company's social media pages. Most companies have social media pages, and this will give you an in-depth idea of the company's culture. Browsing through the company's social media handles can help you see some red flags about the company. Browsing through the company's posts and the comments will help you make the right decision.

c. Check review websites for more information

You may not find all the information you need to know about the company on their website or their social media pages. A good place to get useful information about a company is to check review websites and search for what employees and other people are saying about the company.

mysalaryscale.com will give you all the information you need to know about the company, show you what people are saying about the company, and also give you an idea of the company's salary structure.

Research the job role

Researching the job role does not mean learning about the job role, because you know the kind of job you are applying for. Researching the role has to do with researching the role in that particular company. You research the role in a particular company to discover the skills that the employer considers important for that role. This will allow you evaluate your capacity to function in that role; this will simply help you know whether or not you should go on with the application.

6.4 TOP JOB INTERVIEW DOS AND DON'TS

A job interview is a time for you to show your prospective employer that you are the best person for the position and that you will also be a good fit for the company as well. To prove this to them, you have to make sure you have what it takes to convince them.

To excel in a job interview, it is important you know the right things to do and say to make that great first impression. It is even most important for you to avoid mistakes that could cost you the chance of getting a job.

Here are some job interview dos and don'ts that will help you succeed in your next interview:

Job interview dos

1. **Be punctual**: Make sure you check the time it will take you to get to the venue before the day. Be there for at least 10-15 minutes before the interview.

2. **Dress appropriately**: Like the popular saying, "dress the way you want to be addressed", your dressing says a lot about you. Always remember to keep it professional.

3. **Research the company:** Researching the company before the day of the interview is one thing that you

should never forget to do. Having a good knowledge of the company will even help you answer the interview questions better.

4. **Be polite**: You should be polite to the people you meet at the venue. You are not supposed to be polite to the interviewer alone, but anyone and everyone you meet there. Greet everyone with a smile. Being polite shows that you would be easy to deal with.

5. **Listen carefully to questions**: When you listen well, you will be able to understand the questions that the interviewer asks you. Listening skills is one skill that employers look out for in prospective candidates.

6. **Express yourself and views clearly**: When answering questions, it is important for you to state your views and opinions very clearly so that the recruiter understands your take on a question very clearly without misinterpretations.

7. **Make eye contact**: You should make eye contact when talking to the interviewer. Eye contact is one of the most important forms of non-verbal communication.

8. **Show enthusiasm**: You have to show the interviewer that you are enthusiastic about the position and working in the company at large. The interviewer needs to see that you are excited about working with them.

9. **Ask questions**: Always look forward to asking the interviewer questions. Asking questions will help you evaluate the company better and to decide if the job is one that you would like to do. It also

shows the interviewer that you are interested in the company in the first place.

10. **Be confident**: Always remember to be confident and not arrogant. Applying for the position means that you can do the job, so you have to be confident about what you can do. Confidence shows to the interviewer that you know what you have.

11. **Make sure you present your skills and abilities**: Be sure to present your skills and abilities to your prospective employer. Even when you are talking about your weakness, present it a way that it appears as a strength. Recruiters are interested in the value that you are bringing to the company.

12. **Be sure of your career goals**: It is good for you to identify your career goals before the day of the interview. Identify career goals that are in line with the goals of the job or the company at large. The interviewer wants to know how committed you are going to be if you are employed.

13. **Say thank you and follow-up**: You should say thank you after the interview. You should not just say thank you at the end of the interview by word of mouth, you should send a thank you note. It shows your appreciation. It is important for you to follow-up within 7-10 days after the interview.

Job interview don'ts

1. **Don't be untidy:** When going for an interview, don't dress untidily or too casual. It shows that you are not serious. The interview is a corporate meeting, so you need to appear corporate and professional.

2. **Don't lie**: If you lie about your skills and abilities just to get the job, then you are going to find your-

self in a position that you won't like at all or you will find it hard to cope with the position when you are employed.

3. **Don't bring people**: When you are going for an interview, you should go alone. Going with your friends can distract you, and it can also be seen as unprofessional.

4. **Don't interrupt the interviewer**: Don't interrupt your interviewer during the interview. When you interrupt the interviewer every time when they are trying to ask you questions, it can mean that you are not patient and that you are also arrogant.

5. **Don't make a derogatory comment about your previous employer**: If you go on making derogatory remarks about your former boss, the interviewer will assume that you will do the same thing to them some time.

6. **Don't talk about salary or bonus**: During the interview, don't ask about salary or bonuses unless they start the conversation. Asking salary questions too early can mean that you are just after the money and nothing more.

7. **Don't act too desperate**: Even if you have been searching for a job for a very long time, you should never act desperate during the interview. Be sure your skills and qualification are what they need. Never act like you will die if you don't get the job.

8. **Don't show a lack of knowledge about the position and company**: You should always prepare well when you are going for an interview. If you get to the interview venue and show that you have little or no knowledge about the role that you applied for

or the company, it just shows that you are lazy and unserious.

9. **Don't be afraid to ask for clarification**; if you don't understand a question ask for it to be rephrased. It shows that you are patient and careful about how you choose your words. It is important for you to ask for clarification than misunderstand a question and reply wrongly.

6.5 PRACTISING JOB INTERVIEW QUESTIONS AND ANSWERS

Do you remember this old saying; "practice makes perfect"? Well, this is the idiom that you are going to be working with in this section. We are proud of the effort you have put into making your job search a successful one.

Considering the effort that you have put into creating a CV, writing a cover letter and all the knowledge you have about the interview process; it will be an effort in futility to finally get into the interview room and have no clue about what to say, and probably mess up the entire interview.

To prevent all these from happening, you would have to hold on to the magic word of this section; which is practice. Practising the top job interview questions and answers will prepare you for the big day.

In this section, we have put together answers to the top interview questions to make practice easy for you. In this section, we will be addressing questions based on the different types of interviews that we have, which are:

- Behavioral interview questions
- Panel interview questions

- Competency-based interview questions
- Brainteasers
- Traditional interview questions
- Experience -based interview questions
- Opinion based interview questions
- Trap interview questions
- Salary interview questions
- Communication interview questions
- Hypothetical interview questions

Traditional interview questions

Traditional interview questions focus on your skills and value. These kinds of questions are usually very descriptive. It gives the interviewer an idea of who you are, and how you fit into the role and company at large.

Traditional interview questions are usually the first set of questions that an employer will likely ask a job seeker. Traditional interview questions tend to be straightforward questions that focus on your personality, preferred ways of interacting with others and how you would likely act when you get the job.

1. "Tell me about yourself"?

This is one question that you are sure to be asked regardless of the position that you are applying for. This question can take different forms like;

a. Can I meet you?
b. Who are you?
c. Can we know you?

You don't need to be confused they all mean the same thing.

As simple as the question looks, it could also be very tricky. Be careful not to give unnecessary personal details about yourself. All the recruiter wants to know is who you are and how you fit into the role and the company's vision and work environment.

Be careful to frame your response around what makes you the best fit for the role. You might be tempted to talk about all the good stuff, but you will need to keep it concise and relevant.

These statements will guide your response to the question;

- Talk about who you are professionally
- Highlight your competencies
- Talk about why you are here

For instance, if you are applying for the role of a customer service manager, then your response can be something like this;

Sample Answer

"I am an innovative customer service manager with 6 years of experience managing and monitoring all the aspects of the customer service function-from solving customer's problems to ensuring customer retention to increasing sales. (Who you are).

I have spent 6 years developing my skills as a customer service manager. I have been able to attract recognition and several awards even national awards 3 times. I love solving customer problems and overseeing my team members do so too. (Competence highlights)

Even though I love my current position, I know that I am ready to take up a more challenging role in customer service, and that is why I am very excited about this position. (Why you are here)"

You can see that this answer responded to the three statements that we made earlier. You can use the statements to frame your own answer too.

Never give this kind of answer:
"My name is Daniel Peters, I am from Delta state, and I attended St. Johns primary school after which I went to Methodist Boys School. After my secondary education, I gained admission into the University of Lagos. I am from a family of 6, my parents are very poor, and so I need this job so that I can take care of my siblings ..."

2. What are your strengths?
This question could be really confusing and hard to crack most times because you are asked to talk about your strong points. It is quite normal for you to feel awkward talking about your strengths without bragging.

Well, to answer this question effectively, you will have to follow these steps;
- Assess your hard skills
- Assess your transferable skills
- Assess your personal traits

When you are assessing these skills, make sure they are closely related and relevant to the position that you are applying for. When you want to answer, try and stay away from personal qualities and concentrate more on professional traits.

As simple as the question looks, it is also very possible for you to mess the whole interview up especially if you have not taken out the time to discover yourself to know your strengths, and how to properly communicate them to the recruiter.

You should also be able to accurately choose strengths that will help you perform the task well if you are offered the job. It means that you should not have a one fits all answer to this question.

When answering this question, remember that the recruiter is looking for a good fit, and at the same time trying to form a picture of you based on your response, and make sure your strengths are real strengths that will add value to the company. See sample answer to help frame your answer;

If you are applying for the position of a customer service manager, this is what your response will look like:

Sample Answer
"My strength is my patience with solving problems (Assess your hard skills).

In my current position as a customer service manager, I was patient (Personal trait) enough to turn a toxic work environment to a positive one, and created a motivating environment where everyone can work comfortably.

I also feel that my communication skills (transferable skills) are top-level because I relate with senior executives on the same basis that I relate with junior staff members."

This answers the question well to a large extent because the answer highlights the strengths that are relevant to that particular position. The candidate did not only give a well-rehearsed answer but also gave a real-life instance that makes it more detailed.

3. Can you tell us about your weaknesses?

This may sound like the trickiest question that a recruiter can ever ask. It may feel awkward for you to talk about your weakness during a job interview when you are supposed to be pitching yourself. The confusing part of the whole question is how to talk about your weakness, but not making it a big threat to the role that you are applying for.

When recruiters ask this question, they are not very much concerned about the answer, but they are more concerned about how you answer the question. Many candidates tend to lie about their weaknesses; you shouldn't lie about your weakness even if you should put it in a subtle manner.

When you are answering questions about your weakness, you should be careful not to give cliché answers that are not close to being your weakness at all. Avoid answers like "my greatest weakness is that I am so much of a perfectionist, I love everything to be organized and orderly all the time."

This answer looks perfect, but this is a common cliché that sounds really unrealistic and doesn't reflect a true weakness at all.

The tips below will guide you to answer this question well:

Be self-aware: To answer this question well, you have to be self-aware to recognize your real weakness. Be careful when choosing a weakness so that it does not affect your chance of getting the job.

Be truthful: As much as you want to give a piece of information that will not your job, you should also be sure that you are talking about a real weakness.

Self-improvement/recovery: After telling the recruiter about your weakness, you should also state the effort that you are putting in to manage the weakness that you stated.

Sample Answers

Sample 1

"I am impatient working in a team (self-awareness). I love to work independently and so it is difficult for me to rely on others to complete a task. That is why I have pursued a position that makes it possible for me to work independently (be truthful). However, I have also worked to improve this weakness by enrolling in team building workshops. While I work independently, I must learn to trust my co-workers better." (Self-improvement/recovery).

Sample 2

"Public speaking makes me nervous (self-awareness). Even if I don't have to do too much of public speaking in my role as a graphic designer, I nonetheless feel it is an important skill I have to get used to when communicating with others. (Truthful)

To overcome the fright, I spoke to my manager that I would love to give the introductory speech during our team meetings. This has allowed me to be less nervous speaking to a group of people and has also helped me communicate better with team members to do their jobs effectively." (Self-improvement/recovery)

This answer works well because the candidate mentions a real weakness that does not affect the candidate's ability to do the job. Secondly, the candidate shows the eagerness to develop strategies to tackle the weakness.

4. Why are you leaving your current job?

This is one question that can throw a job seeker off the balance if the person is not very prepared for the question. Many times job-seekers sincerely leave their current jobs because they want to get a better offer, but that is not what you will want to tell your prospective employer.

This question could be really tricky because you don't want to say that you are leaving your current job because you want a better offer and sound like a "gold digger" that will still leave in search for a better offer somewhere else.

To tackle this question, you would need to give an answer that is closely related to you wanting to move forward in your career. No one would frown at anyone's attempt to moving their career forward. You have to be careful not to emit "negative vibes" when answering the question.

You can take a look at these sample reasons that are easy to explain;

- Your desire to improve work/life balance.
- Your wish to learn
- Your yearning to take on more responsibility
- Your wish to take on less responsibility
- Wanting to relocate
- The desire for a career change.
- A desire for career growth and development
- No longer interested in the company's vision and goal.
- Desire for a shorter commute to work.

Answering this question, you should not just throw the answer at the recruiter; you should take time to and make sure you are giving the right answer to the question. You can use this opportunity to talk about your interest in the new position that you are applying for and not talk despairingly about your current employer.

Don't be negative about your current employer; you should rather focus on what the new position will afford you (career-wise). If you speak poorly of your boss during an interview, what proof does the potential employer have that you wouldn't say the same thing about them in another environment?

Always avoid answers that relate to compensation, company finance or poor management. You should always stay positive regardless.

Sample Answers

Sample Answer 1
"I have really learned a lot working with an amazing group of people in my current employment, but this opportunity fits very well with the direction I want to take in my career path."

Sample Answer 2
"I have acquired great experience in my current job, but due to the size of the organization, growth is limited. So for me to continue to grow, I need to go somewhere else, and working in this company will avail me the opportunity to grow in my career."

Remember to be positive and frame your answers around the organization you wish to work for.

5. Why should we hire you?
Most times when recruiters ask this question, job seekers are mostly thrown in a state a confusion. Most times, it is like putting the job seeker in the position of the recruiter. This question will make many job-seekers ask themselves this question; *"If I were the employer, why would I hire myself?"*

Often when recruiters ask *"why should we hire you?"*, they indirectly want to know why you are the best fit for the job.

As straight forward as the question may look, you still have to be very careful when answering the question. Don't be in a hurry to throw the answer back at the recruiter, you might end up giving a negative impression about yourself.

You should always avoid answers like:

"You should hire me because I know you urgently need someone to fill this position, and I think I can do the job".

You need to take your time to think of a concise and effective answer to this question. Before you attempt to answer the question, you should know;

- Why recruiters ask the question
- How to answer the question
- The best response to give

Why recruiters ask "why should we hire you?"

Job seekers may feel that recruiters ask this question just to make them feel uncomfortable, but that is not the case. Recruiters ask this question because they want to know why you are the best fit for the job.

Recruiters simply want to know how you fit into the position they are recruiting for.

How to answer the "why should I hire you question?"

Since the whole interview boils down to this one question, then it is worth preparing for. You should always understand that the interviewer wants to know how you fit into the position. Make sure your response clearly states why you are the best person for the position.

Since every hire is a risk to the recruiter, then you should be ready to prove to the recruiter that;

- You can perform the task excellently.
- You will perfectly fit into the position and be a great addition to the team.
- You possess the right skills and experiences that make you stand out from other candidates.
- Hiring you will add a great deal of value to the company.

Sample Answers

If you are applying for a marketing role;

"From your job advert, I understand that your company is looking for an experienced marketer that will grow the business and help the company stand out from its competitors. At my previous company, I increased the sales by 30% within the space of one year by devising targeted social media advertising strategies. I will bring in that spirit of ownership and innovation to this company if I am given the opportunity."

If you are applying for the role of a web developer;

"I believe that my experience in technology, specifically in web design makes me the best person for this position. In my previous job, I was responsible for updating the company's website. This required me to always make sure everything goes on well on the web page, update employee profile and ensure proper content upload on the site. I enjoyed the role, which was what attracted me to this company; I would love to bring in my skills to this position".

How to answer the question if you are a fresh graduate with no work experience

Getting your first job after graduation may not be as hard as you may think. It is true that employers are keen about getting the right talent to fill their positions, but being a fresh graduate is not a disadvantage if you prepare well for the interview.

If this question comes up in an interview, chances are it will be the only valuable opportunity for you to prove that you are the best candidate for the job.

Remember to stay away from answers that will remind the employer that you have no experience and probably not a good fit, like:

"You know it is really hard to find a job especially when you have no experience, I don't want to stay idle, and I want something that will keep me busy".

This kind of response doesn't show the employer that you have a special interest in the job and the company at all, and you have also succeeded in reminding the employer that you don't have any experience.

Instead of answering like that, you can phrase your answer in such a way that it will show your interest in that particular position, your enthusiasm to be a part of the organization, your interest in learning and development, and your vision to contribute to the overall growth of the company.

Your response should look like this:

"I am a very driven and open-minded person that learns fast. Dur-

ing my volunteer with a local retail outlet, I discovered how much I enjoyed solving customers' problems and rendering service in general. Looking at the job description and what I have learned from the interview, I think this position will support my interest and will also give me the opportunity to contribute positively to the organization, and am very excited about this opportunity".

This kind of answer will give the employer an idea that you are passionate about the position, and a passionate person is someone that can learn fast. Every employer would love to hire someone with the right spirit.

6. Where do you see yourself in 5 years?

This is one question that employers use to trap you in a corner and you may not even recognize it at all. Employers don't just ask this question because they are really interested in what you want to do with your life in 5 years' time. Employers ask this question for two reasons:

- The employer wants to know how long you plan to stay in the position.
- The employer wants to know if your vision aligns with that of the company.

As much as the employer wants know your plan in the position and the company, it could be tempting for you to pour out your sincere intentions, but saying it out like that may not be the best approach to the question.

This is the response that your mind will likely prompt you to give, and it is probably what the interviewer doesn't want to hear:

- Plans about how you would love to take the position of the hiring manager in 5 years.
- Strategies about how you would be promoted in a few years.
- Your aspiration about owning your own business in a few years
- A straight *"I don't know"*, *"I don't have any plans for the*

future, I just want a job now".

I know you would be anxious to ask "then what does the recruiter want to hear?" You should never forget that the business of a recruiter is that he wants to get the right candidate that would stay and grow in the position.

So when recruiters ask *"where do you see yourself in 5 years?"* they simply want to know your career goals within the position.

The hiring manager is interested in knowing how satisfied you are with the position and the company and how long you are willing to grow and stay in the company.

Sample Answers

This is how your answer should look like:

"In 5 years, I would love to complete my internal and external training program for my position. I have read about it on your website, and I think it is an amazing opportunity for me to learn. I don't only look forward to getting the right training for my role, but it will quicken my journey to becoming a marketing manager which is my career goal. My ideal track would be creating awareness in rural areas. I learned that getting products to rural places is one goal this company wants to achieve."

Answering the question like this expresses two things to the employer:

- With this answer, you have given the hiring manager the impression that you are satisfied with the position, and also enthusiastic about developing in the position.
- This answer also shows that your personal career goals align with the company's vision.

More responses

"I am propelled to be the best at what I do, and I want to work in an organization that will allow me to develop my skills, handle interesting projects, and be part of a team that I can learn from. A good number of .creative thinkers in the industry work here, and that is a big

reason why I would love to build a career here".

"My current goal is to fit into a position at a company where I can grow and take on new challenges and responsibilities over time. Moving forward, I would love to assume management responsibility and get involved in pushing the brand. Ultimately, I would love to be a part of an organization where I can build a career".

Since this question is very tricky, you need to be careful not to just speak out words that come to your mind immediately the recruiter asks the question. Be careful not to give answers like: *"I have never settled for less all my life, so in 5 years' time I would be working my way through to becoming the CEO".*

See preparations you should make before attempting to answer the question:

- Know the long term goals that can grow from this position.
- Do a good research on the company and the position to know; the career path for the position, research if there are development opportunities, if there are interesting projects that you would love to be a part of, and finally if you share the same values with the organization.

Always keep the following in mind when you are answering this question:

- No recruiter sincerely cares about what you want to do with your life in the next 5 years, and they don't expect you to have the exact picture of where you are going to be in 5 years.
- Recruiters ask this question because they look forward to getting a hire that would take the role seriously.
- Recruiters want to find out if you would be available for a long time to do the work.

In all sincerity, all a recruiter wants to hear when they ask, "where do you see yourself in 5 years?" is "HERE". As funny as this may sound, this is the truth, employers look forward to getting someone that would love to build their career in the company

7. Can you take a wild guess what salary we might pay someone with your skillset and experience to do the job you applied for?

When interviewers ask this question, they simply want to know how much you expect to get paid in that position without coming out straight. Interviewers want to have an idea of how much a prospective hire would love to get so that they can see if it matches well with what they planned out for that position.

You need to be careful when answering this question because the interviewer is indirectly asking you how much you want to earn.

When you are answering this question, make sure you:
- Research the salary range for your role.
- Give a range and not a clear cut figure.

You should avoid:
- Saying a particular figure.
- Refusing the question outrightly since it is a wild guess.

Sample Answer
"I am looking at a range of 100 – 150, I believe that this is the range that most companies like this will pay someone with my skill and experience".

8. Have you ever been forced to resign?

During an interview, it is quite normal for the recruiter to bring up discussions about your previous employment. One question that the recruiter may likely ask you is if you have ever been forced to resign. The interviewer will likely use your response to the question to know the kind of issue that may likely arise if the company hires you.

The recruiter may also judge your ability to learn from the situation and how much you are able to sincerely account for your actions from your response to the question. When answering this question, you need to be very careful. Keep the following in mind:

- Don't lie about the situation that led to the resignation in your previous employment.
- Do your best to avoid being negative about your experience and try not to bad mouth your previous employer.
- Avoid pushing all the blame of the incident to the organization or the employer. You should try your best to show how some of your actions contributed to the situation.
- Avoid putting yourself in the state of pity that would make everyone else involved wrong. It gives the recruiter the idea that you would repeat the same action again.

This is what you should rather focus on:

- Tell the recruiter about what you have learned from the situation, and how the experience has molded you into a better person.
- Show that you have made an effort to address the action that contributed to you being fired.
- Always let the interviewer know that you have eliminated any action that may make you face the same situation with a new employer.

Sample Answer

This is an example of an answer that will properly deal with this question:

"I was forced to resign because marketing wasn't a strong fit for me. My employer was extremely pleased with my customer service and support skills, but over a long period of time, I wasn't meeting up with

my monthly sales goals. I have decided to shift my focus on customer service and support. This position offers me a better opportunity to leverage on my communication skills".

This question may appear to be one question that you want to avoid. Focusing on the positive angle when answering this question will give you the opportunity to explain that you are the right person for the position.

9. What do you like least about your job?

This question can seem like a net to trap you because the recruiter looks forward to getting a negative response from you, and if you are not careful, you may likely prevent yourself from getting the job.

It is important for you to understand that the interviewer is trying to know if you are going to be satisfied with the position. So if you give the interviewer the impression that you were dissatisfied with your previous job, the interviewer may have the impression that you may also be dissatisfied with the position you applied for.

When you are asked this question, try to be honest with your answers and also maintain a positive tone. This is what you should emphasize when you are about to answer this question:

- Don't mention something you dislike that is common with the position that you are applying for.
- Avoid talking about personal issues you have with co-workers in the office.
- Avoid answers that will make you appear as an incorrigible person.
- Avoid giving the interviewer the impression that you are difficult to please.
- Don't use this question as an opportunity for you to start bad mouthing your previous boss or company.

You should rather look forward to creating an impression that will make the recruiter not scared about you taking up the new position. You can start off your answer by using this approach:

- Mention what you like about your previous job.
- Touch on what you did not like and focus on things you like about the task or a particular situation.
- You can talk about how you were able to manage the situation until you decided to move on in your career.

Sample answers

Sample Answer 1

"I really liked my previous employer and the talented people in my team. One of the challenges that I faced was working remotely from my location, and it became more challenging for me as the company grew bigger. I was also tired of limiting myself to working alone. Why I am enthusiastic about this job is that it will give me the opportunity to work remotely when the need arises. I look forward to connecting with team members physically and not just online"

Sample Answer 2

"I really cannot say I dislike anything about my current job. My company is a start-up that is still in its infantry stage which gives a limited room for advancement. I think I have gotten to the peak of my career in my current organization, and I would like to learn more about technology because the world is becoming technologically based. Regrettably, we don't work with technology-based tools, in order to advance my career, I've decided it is time to move on"

Sample Answer 3

"It is a really great company overall, but my position kept me behind the scenes (I was always in the computer room), with very little interaction with co-workers and customers. I love solving computer or gadget-related problems, but I value human relation a lot too, this is why I am really enthusiastic about this job"

When you are answering this question, be careful not to go on negative about your current job and employer. You should rather use the question as an opportunity to tell the interviewer how the job matches your skills and personality.

10. How would your last boss describe you?

When employers ask this question, they simply want to know what your strengths and weaknesses are. The answer you give will help the interviewer understand why your current employer sees you as a great asset to the team.

These are the points you should focus on when answering the question:

- Relate your answers to why you think you are a good fit for the position.
- You can point out two to three points about how your boss sees your performance.
- Don't forget to state how you enjoyed working with your boss
- You can tell a story about your recommendation with your boss.

You should also avoid making mistakes like:

- Bad mouthing your boss to bring out your good traits.
- Don't spin out negative thought that your boss had about you. Even if there are some negative feelings you should also see the positive light of it.
- Avoid bragging about how well you and your boss went along

Sample Answers

Sample Answer 1

"My last boss would say that I am always proactive and prepared to solve any form of challenge. Nothing takes me unawares, I am usually prepared to face future challenges. I think that my ability to see a problem beforehand and solve them while they are still at the formative stage is what sets me apart from other employees".

Sample Answer 2

"My last boss would see me as a problem solver and when I newly started my past position, I was always ready to face challenges and solve problems with ease. I think that my ability to be calm when there is a difficult situation is what distinguished me from other employees".

Sample Answer 3

"I think my boss would talk about my two most obvious traits which is hard working and result oriented. My boss has always known me as someone that loves things to be done the right way and at the right time. So I was always putting in more hours to make sure that we achieve the desired result in any project. My boss always commended me for that. I also work hard to keep myself up-to-date on current industry trends and technologies by attending meet-ups and workshop to better position myself to face up to any challenge that may arise in the cause of performing my job".

11. Can you give an example of a time that you were pleased with your work (what happened, what was your reaction)?

When an interviewer asks you this question, the interviewer simply wants to understand what success means to you. Simply put, the interviewer wants to have an idea of your definition of success and a feel of what brings satisfaction to you. The interviewer also wants to know how much concern you have for the growth of the company.

When answering this question, focus on:
- What exactly you did.
- The actions you took that led to success.
- Why you were pleased with the actions.
- The effect your actions had.

Avoid:
- Bragging
- Exaggeration

Sample Answers

Sample Answer 1

"I was handling a project to do a blog post that would inspire people. So I did a research on topics that people will be interested in and topics that can help people become better. I asked a couple of friends about their suggestion and I started the post. I also reached out to CEO's that could be a source of inspiration to others. When we published the post, we discovered that we got far more recognition than what we planned for initially and we received an enormous turn out of testimonials that affected our sales that year. I was very pleased with the approach that I took to make that project a success".

Sample Answer 2

"In my first job, I was working as a sales intern, but I was really interested in pushing my sales skills to the next level. I told my supervisor to allow me to sell a product on my own without any guidance or assistance. She agreed, so I did my research, used my internet and PR skills to sell over 90% of the product that I was given. I was really pleased with the fact that I was able to achieve that level of success even with my limited access as an intern".

12. Can you give an example of a time that you solved a problem?

When interviewers ask this question they are really interested in how you go about solving a problem. The interviewer looks forward to understanding your problem solving skills to know how well you will deal with challenges on the job.

How to answer this question
- Identify the problem.
- Clearly explain the method you used to solve the problem.
- Why you decided to use the approach.
- What the solution to the problem was eventually.

Sample Answers

Sample Answer 1

"In my role as the growth lead in my previous company, I was in

charge of managing the growth of the company and to make sure that everything that will finally lead to increased revenue is functioning well. At a point, I noticed that our growth was limited to just one source (online source) and this was limiting the revenue capacity that we would have gotten over time.

Our offline activities were declining fast, and according to my research, I noticed that a better portion of our revenue can best be tapped into from offline activities within our niche. So I called to talk to our sales and marketing team to see how best we can handle the situation. We agreed and came up with offline branding and a lot of PR strategies to put our brand in front of people's eyes. After a while, we noticed that we now had a good number of walk-in request and this increased our client base and revenue too"

Sample Answer 2

"In my role as the Human resources manager, I was responsible for staff welfare and management. During the course of my work, I noticed that we were finding it difficult to get the best candidates for our positions and that of clients. This became a big problem because this was the service that we provide to customers and not getting it right would have an effect on our reputation.

I called a meeting with other Human Resource executives and we tried to find out what we are not doing well, and how fast we can get candidates to clients as early as possible. After series of deliberations, we discovered that we don't search for our candidates the right way, so we decided to add a page to our website where we can have the database of candidates for different positions. We also decided to use online tools like LinkedIn to search for candidates. We found out that we wait till there is so much pressure to start headhunting for talents, so we decided that we will start processing the candidate request as soon as a request is made. All the reformation helped us get candidates faster and also retained our clients".

13. How do you describe your dream company?

When interviewers ask you this question, don't be in a hurry to spill out that dream of working in a company that will be able to pay you six figures, access to expensive vacation, flexible work hours. All these are not what the interviewer wants to hear. The interviewer wants to hear something that will convince him that you are the right person for the job.

You should take note of the following when you want to attempt this question:

- Be sincere about what an ideal workplace is for you.
- Make sure that your dream aligns with that of the company.
- Pay attention to what you can offer the company too.

You should also avoid the following:

- You should avoid exaggeration, avoid saying that this is the best job when it is not
- Avoid citing a specific employer as an example it might be risky

Sample Answer 1

"For me, my dream company is one that will help me better harness my skills and abilities to contribute to the overall success of the company. I value a company that will recognize and appreciate excellent performance".

Sample Answer 2

"My dream company is one where I can contribute to the success of the company. A place that I can get new opportunities that will help me better make use of my skills and abilities. An ideal company will also be one that will provide me with the opportunity to grow my career".

14. How do you set your job goals?

This question can be very easy to answer since it is straight forward. Many times interviewers ask this question because they want to know how organized you are, and they also want to know how you set your goals or if you have any goals at all.

When you are answering this question, you should focus on:

- Your practical approach to setting your job goals
- A hint about why you set your job goals

You should also avoid not being specific with your response to the question

Sample Answer

"I set my job goals by carefully examining my tasks, both short and long term tasks, understanding what result is expected from those tasks, and how I intend to carry out the task. Before I start performing the entire task for a particular day, I look at the task according to their level of importance. I start with a smaller task with a small goal so that there would be room for progression. I set my job goals with the expected result in mind".

15. How do you deal with stress?

Employers know that everyone feels stressed at one point or the other while performing their task. So when you are asked interview questions about how you deal with stress, the interviewer does not expect you to say that you don't feel stressed. The interviewer only wants to know how stress affects you and how you go about dealing with it.

When you are answering this question, you pay attention to the following:

- Give an example of how you have handled stress well in the past.
- Talk about a stressful situation that is related to the work.
- Walk the interviewer through how you managed stress previously.

You should avoid doing the following:

- Talking about a stressful situation that is not related to the job.
- Talking too much about the stress rather than how you were able to manage it.
- Giving answers like this *"I never feel stressed"*

Sample Answers

"I know that sometimes it is hard to avoid stress, but I try to face the situation, rather than being stressed. Regardless of how much work I have to do, I make sure that I tackle the situation rather than being overwhelmed by the problem. That way, I handle the situation better and don't get stressed. For example; when I dealt with an un-satisfied customer that was angry and was ready to give a negative review about our product. Instead of feeling stressed, I concentrated on finding out what her challenge was exactly and looked for ways to help her get the problem solved, addressing it to the right channel. My ability to remain calm when dealing with the unsatisfied customer reduced my stress and the stress that the customer may face".

16. Tell us about what you have done to prepare for this job

It is the goal of every employer or hiring manager to find the best hire that will fit into the position for which they are hiring. The interviewer will likely ask a candidate this question in an interview to find out if the candidate understands to a large extent the job he/she is applying for.

Since hiring managers look forward to hiring candidates that have the highest level of qualification, skill, and experience to perform the job. The candidate's response should reflect that he/she has the right education, qualification, skill, and experience to perform the job.

When answering this question, you should focus on the following:

Your response should show that you understand the job that you applied for.

Talk about courses and training that will help you perform the job better.

Show how your experience makes you the best person for the job.

You should avoid the following:

- Talking about your skills and achievements that

make you the best person for the job.
- Not talking about other things that makes you the best person for the position.

Sample Answer 1

"Preparing for this position is one of the most important things that I have prepared for all my life. From a young age, I have known that I would be doing something that has to do with people even if I had not discovered it. As I grew older, I was able to identify that I was interested in employment/recruitment and personnel management.

"Understanding the role that humans play in the work chain, I decided to study Human Resources and Personnel management as an undergraduate. Taking it further, I obtained my Master's Degree in Human Resources and Personnel management. Meeting with other professionals and knowing the core of Human resource practice is important in the practice. I took a certificate course in Human resources and personnel management.

While getting the required knowledge to perform excellently as a Human Resource manager, I have also gained over 8 years of experience in Human Resource practices. With over 4 years of experience working as a human resource manager in a manufacturing company, I know that it won't be challenging for me to perform this role effectively".

Sample Answer 2

"For me, communication is key to addressing a stressful situation. Many times I communicate as much as possible to make sure that I am on the same page with everyone involved in what I am working on. It reduces errors and cuts down stress to a very large extent. In my previous job, I was working on a project with another team and found out that after a while we had a different approach on the same project. I called for a stand-up meeting so that we can come to a logical conclusion and carry on with the project. At the end of the day, we agreed on one vision and the project went on successfully".

17. What do you like most about your last job?

This kind of interview question is really tricky; you should be careful not to talk yourself out of the job. Remember to be honest whenever you are asked this question. While you are trying to be honest, you should also keep your response on the positive side.

One major reason why interviewers ask this question is to know if you are going to be happy and satisfied with the job. Every employer looks forward to working with people that will be happy and satisfied with their jobs. So if you were not satisfied performing the same role in another company, the hiring manager will simply believe that you will not be satisfied performing the role in the company too.

You should take note of the following when you are answering this question:

- Give an example of things that you enjoyed in your previous job.
- Make sure that what you choose to talk about is related to the position that you are applying for.
- Make sure that your answer is direct and straight to the point.

You should also avoid the following:

- Giving an example that may water down your abilities. Examples like *"I enjoyed my previous job because I usually have little or nothing to do most times"*
- Sharing an irrelevant experience like *"I enjoyed the fact that my team members were all very beautiful ladies"*.
- Exaggerating things from your last job.

Sample Answer 1

"In my previous job, I really enjoyed the fact that the company is enthusiastic about employees' growth as much as I am passionate about my career growth. Within the first 3 years of my stay in my previous job, I had taken several content development training all of which helped me develop my skills in content development. Both the

internal and external training has helped me move up my career ladder as the team lead for content development in the company. I really enjoyed the fact that there was an opportunity for growth"

Sample Answer 2

"Before my last employment, I have always looked forward to working in an environment that supported teamwork to a large extent. In my last job, I was a member of the IT team and we handled both internal and external project. I usually enjoy the fact that we handle different bits of the project, and at the end, we come together and those tiny bits will become one whole amazing project. The integration of people to achieve a goal is what appeals to me in my last job, and that is why I am enthusiastic about this job too".

18. Do you think you're qualified for this position?

During an interview, the interviewer can ask you questions like; why do you think you are the best person for this? Or why should we hire you?

Interviewers ask this question because they want to know why they should hire you over every other candidate. So while you are trying to answer this question, you should focus on things that make you the best person for the position. Emphasize your skills, your abilities, and experience to emphasize that you are the best person for the position.

When you are answering this question, you should focus on:
- Your skills and abilities that match that of the company.
- How you wish to help the company achieve its goal.
- Showing the interviewer that you are interested in the position.
- Picking a valuable skill that will set you apart from other candidates. A skill that will help you perform excellently in the job.

You should also avoid the following:
- Avoid focusing more on your personality rather

than the skill.
- Avoid watering down your skills and experiences.
- Avoid bringing down other candidates.

Sample Answer 1

"My 6 years of experience in customer service has given me insight into what your customer service job entails. I am a very result-driven person, and my enthusiasm for problem-solving has motivated me to do more as a customer service person and also to help my team members achieve more. During my stay at my previous job, I was able to manage a team of 50 customer service representatives. Building enthusiasm among my team members and motivating them to achieve results is what made us stand out among other teams in my company".

Sample Answer 2

"In my previous role as a marketer, I have taken almost every responsibility in the marketing department. I managed and optimized the company website, social media marketing, physical marketing, and PR. Because of my vast knowledge in almost every aspect of marketing, I know that I can bring in that same unique skill into this position".

19. What are your weaknesses?

Interview questions about your weaknesses are questions that candidates hate the most. Candidates feel uncomfortable with the question because they know that everyone has a weakness. But how would you talk about your weakness without looking like a terrible candidate for the job?

The best way to answer this question is minimizing the weak traits and emphasizing the positive angle to it. While you point out a weakness, it is equally important that you talk about how you plan to manage it.

You can take these steps to answer the question:
Think about something that you are not very good at in the past.

Look at steps you have taken to put that in check. Emphasize that you are working on becoming better.

You should also avoid the following:
- Lying
- Giving answers like "I don't have a weakness"

Sample Answer 1

"Well, I used to have a problem setting priorities. I usually accept any task that comes to me without even considering if I could do it or not. So at the end of the day, I try my best to complete all the task and most times I find myself stressed out without even completing the task and the most important task suffer.

So considering the problem, I took a course in time management where I learned how to manage my time effectively. Now, I put priorities on the bigger projects and tasks before attending to other ones. Even if I still take up more task, I have learned to a great extent, how to prioritize well".

Sample Answer 2

"Well, I used to be not so good at public speaking, I get really nervous when I am in the front of people and I knew it was a problem I was supposed to fix. I decided that I would make myself available when there is an opportunity to speak to a group of people. So I decided to give a short speech before every team meeting. I also enrolled in a public speaking class to help speak better in public. During our last conference, I spoke to about 1000 people even though I still felt a little bit uneasy and I was greatly congratulated".

20. What is the most significant thing you learned at your last job?

Employers are usually interested in employees that can learn easily. Being able to identify the things that you have learned in your previous job will give the interviewer the mindset that you are teachable and that you are willing to learn.

It is important for you to note that the interviewer wants to learn how your experiences in your last job were for you. It does not matter if it was positive or negative. The interviewer just wants to know how you turn experiences into learning projects.

When you want to answer this question, you should:
- Focus on the positive side of the situation
- Provide a specific example
- Think about the things that you have learned in your previous job that is related to this
- Always remember to stay positive

You should also avoid the following:
- Don't talk down on your previous employment.
- Don't admit that you did not learn anything.
- Avoid keeping quiet when you are asked the question.

Sample Answer 1

"I have always been used to working all by myself and that is because I am a freelancer. Working in my previous company made me learn the importance of teamwork and collaboration. In my previous job, we worked as a team and as a team we were able to achieve a lot together".

Sample Answer 2

"In my previous job, I learned to communicate well. Over the years, I got used to working on my own with little or no communication with others. When I got to my previous job I had to communicate with people to understand their ideas. Since communication is key to every business, I have learned to communicate better".

6.6 DEALING WITH TOUGH INTERVIEW QUESTIONS

There is no doubt that some interview questions may come out as difficult, so the question is what do you do about these kinds of questions?

It may not be possible for you to run away from questions that appear to be difficult simply because they are difficult. The best solution is to look out for the best strategies to tackle difficult questions in case they arise.

Thinking about possible difficult interview questions even before the interview and taking time to tailor the right answers to these questions and finding out strategies to help you answer these questions will go a long way towards making you stand out during your interview process.

Some of the most difficult interview questions are questions that makes job candidates think about their answers critically and creatively. Do you know the interesting part of these difficult questions?

The interesting thing about these questions is that they are quite common. They are part of the questions that we have already answered. Is this not amazing? To make sure you don't forget these seemingly difficult questions, we will quickly list them down here:

- What are your biggest weaknesses?
- Where do you see yourself in 5 years?

- How much do you expect to get paid?
- Why should I hire you?
- Why do you think you are the best person for this position?
- How do you deal with stress?
- How can you describe your dream company?
- What did you like least about your previous job?
- Why are you leaving your job?
- Can you take a wild guess what salary we might pay someone with your skill set and experience to do the job you applied for?

How to respond to difficult questions that you are not prepared for

Since you are going for an interview, then there are chances that questions that you are not exactly prepared for might be thrown at you. We have given you answers to the top 20 interview questions, but are these all the questions that you would be asked during your interviews?

The answer to this question is no! Some hiring managers prefer to ask specific and personal questions instead of the general questions based on their requirement for the position they are looking to hire for. Most times, these questions can come off as difficult; this is why it is good you learn how to deal with them. Now that you know that the recruiter can ask you questions that you did not prepare for, it is time for you to learn how to prepare yourself to answer these questions even before you are asked.

These steps are all you need to tackle impromptu questions during your interviews:

Prepare for possible questions before your interview

Preparing for possible interview questions before your interview will go a long way to preparing you for the interview. Just like we have looked at some possible questions that the recruiter will ask you during your interview, it may not be possible for you to get all the answers to every job interview questions in your head.

Since it is not possible to learn all the answers to all the interview questions recruiters will ever ask, it is also easy for you to prepare for every question that a recruiter will likely ask you by breaking them down into categories.

Regardless of the numbers of interview questions that recruiters likely ask, all these questions can be grouped into categories to help you respond to them even faster.

The interview questions that recruiters ask mostly revolves around the following categories. Preparing a broad answer for the categories will help you answer specific questions that you did not prepare for better.

Behavioural interview questions

In behavioral interview questions, the interviewer focuses on how you were able to handle different work situations in the past. Your answer will reflect your skills, abilities, and personality.

Competency based interview questions

Competency-based interview questions are questions that check your competencies in the position that you are applying for. Competencies like skills, abilities, behaviors, and knowledge of the position that you are applying for are things that will be checked for when asked a competency-based question. Interviewers will likely ask you open questions to discover how you use your competencies in a given real-life scenario. Employers use competency-based interview questions to predict a candidate's future performance.

Brain teasers

Brain teasers are questions that are abstract. This kind of question will require you to come up with a good answer based on logic and analysis. Interviewers use this kind of question to check your problem solving abilities through your thought process. Most times, the interviewer does not expect you to get the answers right at once.

Employers that use brain teasers interview questions are employers that are interested in knowing your approach to solving a problem and your creativity. Often times, IT-related companies use brain teasers to understand the candidate's analytical skills.

Experience-based interview questions

In Experience-based interview, the candidate is made to answer questions about his or her actions in a past employment situation. The interviewer is looking forward to hearing the candidate describe his or her skills, achievement and experience and how they emphasize him/her as the best fit for the position.

Hiring managers use this question to assess if the candidate for the position possess the right skills and abilities that are needed to perform the job using the candidate's experience as a yardstick for measurement.

Trap interview questions

Trap interview questions just as the name suggests are interview questions that aim to stir up the applicant to respond to uncomfortable and unexpected questions. In this kind of interview questions, the interviewer is more interested in your approach to the question rather than your response.

Opinion interview questions

Opinion-based interview questions sometimes seek to know your stand on a particular issue in the workplace or in your job field.

Know the candidate's attitude towards the role.
Know a candidate's attitude towards the company.
Measure a candidate's management skills.

Ask Yourself These Two Questions Before You Respond to Any Questions.

Just like we said earlier that you may not be able to learn and prepare for all the questions that your prospective employer may ask you, but you can come up with strategies and tactics that will help you tackle difficult questions that may arise during the process of the interview.

When you are in front of your recruiter during an interview, you may not be able to tell the kind of questions that the recruiter will ask you. No matter the questions that the recruiter may ask you, it is important for you to ask yourself these questions:

a. Who is asking the question?

Having a clear understanding of who is asking the question will go a long way to helping you organizing your words in such a way that the person will be able to understand you clearly. The fact that you know that it is the recruiter that is asking you the question will guide your response to a large extent.

b. Why is the person asking this question?

Have you ever asked yourself why people ask questions? No matter how dumb a question may appear, it is definitely for a reason. Going for an interview, you sure know that the recruiter is going to ask you some questions.

Knowing why a recruiter is asking you a question will guide your answer to the question. If you have taken out time to go through this chapter, then you would notice that we have been giving reasons why recruiters may ask all the interview questions that we have answered.

Give Yourself Time to Think

Interviews can take time, but it is also good for you to take out time to think through the question before answering them. Being in a hurry to answer the questions may not give you enough time to understand the intent of the question.

It is good you take your time to understand the question and reason why the interviewer is asking the question before you make an attempt to answer the question.

Whatever the Question is, Don't Lie

It could be quite tempting for you to want to be of your best behaviour during an interview. You want to give the right impression, and you also want to be able to answer every question that the recruiter will ask intelligently.

Even if you desperately need a job, you don't have to lie when answering the recruiter's question, you know why? It is simply because you may not know why the recruiter is asking the question. So if you lie, you may just be shooting yourself on the foot. It is better you admit that you don't have an idea about a question than to lie in an attempt to answer a question.

Questions to Ask Your Interviewer During an Interview

It is common for job seekers to see the interview as a time to answer questions that the recruiter will throw at them. So, they can't wait for the recruiter to ask all the questions he wants to ask and move on with their lives.

This is a wrong mindset. As much as the interview is a time for the recruiter or the employer to meet you, it is also a time for you to get to meet with the recruiter and find out more about the company.

All interviewers will allow you to ask questions, and this is an opportunity for you to show that you are interested in the company. Don't mess up this opportunity by giving a response like; *"I don't have any question".*

Asking carefully crafted intelligent questions will emphasize your interest in the job; it can also be a pointer to good character traits the recruiter might be looking out for. Before you ask a recruiter any question, be sure the question will help you achieve the following:

- Leave a positive impact and a great impression on the recruiter/interviewer.
- Allow the recruiter to have a good understanding of your background and qualification.
- Help you get enough information that will help de-

termine if the job is for you.

List of questions you can ask the recruiter:

a. Questions about the hiring process

- What is the next step after this interview process?
- How long does your recruitment process take?
- If I get hired for this position, what is the ideal starting date?
- Can you tell me more about the role, asides what is on the job description?
- When can I expect to hear from someone about this job?
- Who should I get in touch with after the interview?
- How should I contact you?
- If I don't hear from you, what should be the best time to call back?
- How will I be notified if I get the job?
- When will I hear about the result?
- What will the onboarding process be like?

b. Questions about the position

- How does this position contribute to the organization's success?
- What does a typical day look like?
- What would my first week at work look like?
- Can you show me examples of projects I'd be working on?
- What are the skills and experiences you're looking for in an ideal candidate?
- What would my day-to-day routine look like if I got the job?
- What attributes does someone need to have to be successful in this position?
- What types of skills is the team missing that you're looking to fill with a new hire?
- What are the biggest challenges that someone in

this position would face?
- What sort of budget would I be working with?

c. Questions about the company

- Can you describe your work environment here?
- What are the prospects for growth?
- What is the work culture like here?
- How would you describe the overall style of management at the company?
- How does senior management view/interact with the person in this position?
- What do you/employees like most about working here?
- Is there a career path that someone in this position would be expected to follow?
- How does the position fit with the rest of the organization?
- How long does the average person keep this job?
- What model does the company use to correct and instruct?

d. Questions to ask about the interviewer

- How long have you been in the company?
- What do you like most about your job?
- What do you like most about working in this company?
- Can you say that you have grown in this company so far?
- Has your role changed since you have been here?
- Why did you decide to work for this company?
- If there is anything you would love to change about your role, what would it be?
- Have you experienced any challenges performing your role?
- What are the challenges you have to deal with day-to-day that the person in this role should solve?

- What are you most excited about in this company's future?

Recruiters always look forward to answering questions from job seekers, so not asking a recruiter any question maybe you cheating on yourself. You can rob yourself off your dream job by merely failing to ask the recruiter any question.

As good as it may be to ask the recruiter questions during the interview, it is also good for you to pay attention to the questions that you are asking. Some questions can irritate the recruiter and will even reduce your chances of getting a job instead of increasing it.

If you believe in the saying that: "there is no wrong or stupid question" then we think it is time for you to start questioning that believe when it comes to job interviews. When it comes to job interviews, you should not ask the recruiter questions like:

- How did I do in this interview?
- What does this company do?
- If I get the job, can I go on vacation?
- So, did I get the job?
- When can I get an offer for the job?
- How much will I earn if I get the job?
- How often does this company give out raises?
- What kind of benefits can I expect if I get the job?

Even if you have done well during your interview, asking the wrong questions can ruin all your effort of getting the job that you have been looking for.

Another wrong way of asking the questions is by asking too many questions. Asking too many questions gives the impression that you have not researched the company at all.

So, you need to keep the questions short, relevant and straight to the point. As soon as you notice the recruiter is not interested anymore, you can hold on with your questions.

Always remember not to overstay your welcome, it can make the recruiter disinterested in you.

6.7 JOB INTERVIEW PREPARATION CHECKLIST

Now, that you know what the job interview is all about, it is time for you to prepare yourself for the big day; which is the day of the interview. It may not be enough to know what the interview process is all about, but it is good to have something to guide you on the go.

If you have never gone for a job interview, then having a job interview checklist will be helpful as you prepare for a job interview on the go. This job interview checklist is all you need to keep up during your job interview preparation.

Before the day of the interview, you should do the following;

- Research the organization, browse the company website and search for them on the internet.
- Research the industry and job role if it is your first experience or if you are changing career.
- Prepare answers to common interview questions. (Find answers to common Job interviews and answers).
- Make sure you know the name of the person interviewing you.
- Be sure of the interview format or style (whether it is a one-on-one or a panel interview).
- Prepare the cloth you are going to wear.
- Ask a family or friend to do a mock interview with

you
- It is important for you to prepare well to avoid stress.
- Research your interviewers, search for them on LinkedIn and find out more about them.
- Create a well-tailored CV if it is your first time. You can also get a CV template to guide you while writing your CV.
- Print a copy of your CV.
- Go along with your portfolio or where it can be found (maybe an online platform)
- Re-read your CV to be sure there are no errors or conflicting information.
- Plan your journey and determine the distance days before the interview to avoid being late
- Browse your route online and print out a map to be sure
- Get the company's contact number in case you encounter any problem.
- Leave your house about 30 minutes before the time of the interview (depending on the distance).

On the day of the interview, you should do the following:
- Always remember to greet the receptionist or the first person you see at the interview venue to make a good first impression.
- Fill in any form that may be given to you neatly and accurately.
- Greet the recruiter or interviewer with a big smile, calling his or her name or title. Shake hands with the interviewer firmly and avoid a weak handshake that may show a lack of confidence and weakness.
- Be aware of your posture and body language all the time. Make sure you sit only when you are asked to sit.
- Make good eye contact with the interviewer.

- When you are asked a question, avoid beating around the bush, rather go straight and answer the question. Don't let any surprise question take you off balance.
- Avoid using poor language, slang or pause words often.
- Make sure your words and speech suggest that you are enthusiastic about the position and the company
- Maintain high confidence and energy level during the interview, but avoid being rude (sometimes being confident can be perceived as being rude)
- Avoid statements or conversations that suggests desperation
- Remember to stress your achievement and avoid bringing up or stressing personal issues
- You can use a short pause before responding to a question, avoid repeating words and using long pauses.
- Avoid answering a question with a simple "Yes" or "No" response, but you should give adequate information and examples where necessary.
- Don't answer phone calls during the interview, in fact, put your phone on silence or better still, switch it off.
- Avoid demanding from the company, rather show what you can do for the company
- Answer salary questions intelligently
- Ask intelligent questions about the job role, field or industry.
- Ask when you can expect to hear back.

After the Interview, you should do the following:
- Email or send a letter to the interviewer to thank him/her for the opportunity. Sending a thank you note shows that you are passionate and will be com-

mitted to the position.
- Await the answer.
- If you have not been contacted, it is important for you to follow up.
- If you did not get the job, let them know politely that you are still interested; you can also ask them what they think you can do to make you a better candidate for the position.
- Avoid becoming a pest and a disturbance in your attempt to follow up. There are better ways to follow up.

Thank You Note After an Interview

A thank you note template is shared below

Dear Mr./Ms Last Name,
I appreciate your time and the information you shared during the interview on the (date) for the (job title) position. I was pleased to learn more about the company and to also see that the company is interested in (your passion).
I believe my experience as a (what you do) will enable me contribute to the vision of this company.
Please contact me if you have any questions. I look forward to hearing from you soon. Thank you once again for your time.

Regards,
(Your full name)

If you are a little bit confused about how to write a thank you note, then this sample is all you need to guide you through the process.

Samuel Ajayi
2, Obafemi Awolowo Road,
Ikeja, Lagos.
March 4, 2020.

John Gold
Human Resources Manager,
ABC Group of Companies,
5, Admiralty Way, Lekki,
Lagos.
March 4, 2020.

Dear Mr. John,
I just want to thank you for taking out time to invite me to your office today. It was really an amazing time for me today; it was good to hear that ABC Group of companies is focusing on taking children off the street with the launching of ABC Group of Company's Foundation.

I was extremely pleased to learn that the company is ready to invest both its finances and resources to make sure the goal of the Foundation is properly communicated.

ABC Group of Companies Foundation feels like a great place to work, not just because of the benefits you mentioned. I am also passionate about the goal that drives the Foundation, and I look forward to working with the communication team to implement some the ideas we discussed.
Please don't hesitate to contact me if you need any more information.

Regards,
Samuel Ajayi

6.8 CHAPTER ASSESSMENT

We have finally come to the end of this chapter, and as usual, you will have to take an assessment to be sure you have a good grasp of what you have learned so far.

This job interview assessment will help you plan for your interview in the future. You know what they say about planning for the future right? Those who plan stand a greater chance at reaching their destination compared to those who merely swing into action.
So, this is why it is important for you to take the assessment. In this assessment, you will have to provide answers to the questions on the left hand.

The amazing thing about this assessment is that you already have most of the answers. If you have been taking all the chapter assessment in this book, then you are good to go..

Assessment Questions	Answers	Rating (0 -5)
1. Write a list of 3 people that have influenced you. a. _____ b. _____ c. _____		
2. Write a list of 3 things you value the most. a. _____ b. _____ c. _____		
3. Write down 5 skills that you possess. a. _____ b. _____ c. _____ d. _____ e. _____		
4. Give 3 instances where you have demonstrated these skills in the past. a. _____ b. _____ c. _____ d. _____ e. _____		

Figure 6.8.0 *Skill assessment exercise. Use the table above to assess your skills.*

Assessment Questions	Answers	Rating (0 -5)
5. Write down 3 things you want to achieve in this year. (short term goals). a. _____ b. _____ c. _____		
6.Write down 3 things you want to achieve in 5 years (Mid-term goals). a. _____ b. _____ c. _____		
7. Write down 3 things you want to achieve in 10-20 years (long-term plan). a. _____ b. _____ c. _____		
8. Write down 3 things you don't mind doing even if you are not going to get paid for it. a. _____ b. _____ c. _____		

Figure 6.8.1 *Skill assessment exercise. Use the table above to assess your skills.*

Assessment Questions	Answers	Rating (0 -5)
9. Write down 5 things that you have achieved that you feel good about. a. _____ b. _____ c. _____ d. _____ e. _____		
10. List 3 of your recent jobs (this include internships, summer jobs, volunteer experience, etc.). a. _____ b. _____ c. _____		
11. Write down 5 things that you have achieved that you feel good about. a. _____ b. _____ c. _____ d. _____ e. _____		

Figure 6.8.2 *Skill assessment exercise. Use the table above to assess your skills.*

This was easy right? Now that you are done with this, then you must have discovered yourself enough to go for a job interview and kill it. Since you have discovered yourself the more, it is time for you to take the next assessment.

From your response to the questions in the first assessment and your ratings, write down the things that are important for you to get in your next job.

10 Things that Are Important for Me to Get in My Next Job

1.

2.

3.

4.

5.

6.

7.

8.

9.

10.

Figure 6.8.3 *Job assessment. Write down what you expect to see in your new job in the table above.*

Most likely, you have a question on your mind. You might be thinking; "Will I get everything I am seeking in my next job from the list I have made?"

It is understandable that you may likely not get the all the things you are expecting in your next job looking at the list that you just made. The good thing about the list that you made is that it will serve as a guide for your next interview and also as a "blueprint" for evaluating jobs.

This list will also help you assess each job opportunity even before you apply for the job according to your needs. This can also be a source for questions you can ask the recruiter during the interview.

6.9 CHAPTER SUMMARY

Congratulations! You are finally done with your job search journey. With the assessments and all what you have read in this chapter, you are definitely ready to land the job of your dreams sooner than you expect. Is this not amazing already?

The interview stage is the final stage of job search. Excelling at this stage of your job search means that you are definitely prepared to get that position in your dream company.
We are happy that you have gotten all your job search tools right and you are ready to start making a difference in your career.

The aim of this chapter is to help you get a good grasp of the job interview, the processes, and all you need to excel at a job interview. If you have carefully gone through this chapter, then you must have achieved all we listed above.

In the subsequent chapter, we are going to be talking about getting an offer and how to go about your first days at work.

CHAPTER 7

GETTING A JOB OFFER AND YOUR
FIRST 30 DAYS ON THE JOB

It is surely an amazing feeling to find out that all your job search efforts (evaluating yourself, writing a CV, writing a cover letter, and preparing for an interview) have finally paid off. Yes, it has paid off because a recruiter just handed you a job offer. Exciting right?

Well, after you must have yelled and shouted out of happiness because you have finally landed a job, what next? We know the response on your mind is; accept the offer of course.

Well, you may want to accept an offer on the spot because you are excited a recruiter has decided to make you an offer in the first place. Before you shout yes, you should ask yourself the following questions:

a. Have I evaluated the job and organization carefully?

b. Do I know all I need to know about the job conditions?

c. Is this position right for me at this time in my career?

d. Am I really happy and enthusiastic about the job?

If you are clear and sure that you have answered all the questions above, then you can go ahead to say yes to the offer.

If you feel a bit uncertain about the position and the company, don't feel the pressure to accept the offer because you have invested a lot or may be because the recruiter is sitting in front of you. At this point, you can request that the recruiter gives you some time to think about it.

When you do this, don't forget to give the recruiter the specific time you think would be enough for you to think through the offer. You should also not forget to communicate your interest and enthusiasm to the interviewer to reassure them of your interest.

When you request for some time to think about the offer, make sure you are not taking too much time (12 hours is okay). Don't forget to keep up with the agreed time frame.

It may not be easy for you to evaluate the offer if you don't know what to check for. In the next section, we are going to look at how you can evaluate a job offer before saying yes!

7.1.EVALUATING THE JOB OFFER

Searching for a job could be quite overwhelming, and finally getting an offer can bring out all the excitement you never thought you had. Knowing that you finally emerged as the chosen one can even be more exciting.

As exciting as this may be, it can come with some form of worry. Yes, you may worry that if you don't say yes to the offer immediately, you might end up missing out on the opportunity.
It is wise for you not to allow the excitement of the offer to drive you into making a rash decision. Evaluating a job offer takes time and watchful consideration. You don't want to accept a job that seems awesome, only to find out a few days after that the work environment is not something that you can thrive in, the commute is 2 times what you are used to, and you also have to spend long hours in a tiny cubicle.

Before you accept an offer, take a moment to look at the big picture. Don't forget to take a deep look at the list you had made earlier about what you would like or need in your next job. This list will go a long way to guide you in your decision making.
You would have to consider these factors to effectively evaluate a job offer:

a. The paycheque
Money is most probably the first thing you consider to decide if you would accept an offer or not. Once you are offered a salary, take a deep look at your budget to see if that salary is enough

for you. Don't just look at the figure, look at all the expenses you would to make (transportation, feeding, etc.) and then deduct them from the salary.

Doing this will help you realize how much you would be left with every month, and from here you can decide if the salary will work for you or not.

If after deducting all the expenses and you notice that you still have enough for saving and retirement, then you can consider accepting the offer.

Asides your main salary, you can also look at other financial benefits that will make life much easy for you. Other benefits like;

- **Bonuses**: Did you hear anything about bonuses? Is there an opportunity for you to earn performance-based bonuses?

- **Health Insurance and wellness benefits**: Is there a plan for health insurance and wellness? How much is the premium you will have to pay? Is it expensive in comparison with what other companies' pay?

- **Retirement**: Is there a retirement plan? How much will your contribution be towards the retirement plan? What percentage does the employer have to contribute to the retirement plan?

- **Profitsharing**: Does this company practice profit sharing at the end of the year? And if they do, how does it work?

- **Relocation assistance**: If you have to move because of the job, is the company going to pay part of your expenses or some of your expenses?

- **Daycare/child care facility**: Is there an onsite daycare facility or will there be a daycare subsidy?

These are other financial benefits you can consider before accepting an offer, because these benefits may save you the cost of having to directly pay for all of these services from your salary.

b. Company Culture

Have you noticed that people spend their most active hours of the day at work? This also means that you would likely spend more time at work than in your home. Asides the fact that you would have to consider the amount a company is offering; it is also important that you evaluate the kind of environment that you are going to be spending 8-10 hours in.

The salary that a company offers you can be great, but the work environment can be frustrating enough to make you want to leave the job even if you just started.

In evaluating a company's culture, you should take a look at the following:

- **The work environment**: The work environment should be something you should consider before deciding if you would accept the offer or not. Remember you will spend hours in this place, so you have to determine if it is a place you would look forward to going to every day.

You can request for a tour around the office to have a feel of what it will be like working in that environment before you accept the offer.

- **Career development:** Find out if the company offers an opportunity for training and career advancement. You should also be concerned about your growth in the company too. If you accept the offer, is there a possibility that you would grow in say a few months or years to come to a more challenging position?

c. Consider your personal needs

When it comes to accepting an offer, you have to put your personal needs into consideration. It is good you discover the things that are important to you and see how it fits with the job. In as much as the work environment is important, striking a balance between your job and your personal life is also important. Before you accept the offer, you should also consider if the job will allow you to have quality time with your family. Find out if there are travel for fun opportunities

In considering your personal needs, you can find out the following:

- **Travel requirements**: How much travelling will be required of you in the course of the work? Will your personal needs allow you to travel frequently if that is what is demanded from the job? How much of the travelling expenses will be reimbursed?

- **Paid time off**: Find out if the company has any plan for paid time off policies. Are there provisions for leave and leave allowances?

- **Working remotely**: Does working remotely from your home fit with your personal needs. If it does, will this job give you that flexibility?

- Evaluating the offer before accepting it is not what you should do in a hurry. It is good you take your time to evaluate the offer, taking into consideration the factors that we listed above before giving the recruiter an answer.

- Always remember that you would be at the office for a long time, so your decisions concerning accepting the offer should be one that you can cope with as the day goes by working in that company.

You know that every job comes with its own challenges, so it is good you weigh the job and see if the challenges that the job will throw at you are the challenges that you can cope with.

7.2 EVALUATING MULTIPLE OFFERS

As exciting as it might be to finally land a job offer, it could also be even more exciting to find out that you have multiple offers. As overwhelming as it can be to respond to multiple offers, it is also important for you to evaluate all the offers against what you look forward to getting from your next job.

Remember that you have created a list of things you want from your next job earlier, so it is time for you to take a close look at the list to evaluate your offers. Deciding on which offer to settle for when you have multiple offers may not be an easy thing to do, but this assessment will definitely give you heads up as to how to go about evaluating multiple offers.

Job Position Profile

a. Values
Write down 5 of your values that this position fulfills
- _____
- _____
- _____
- _____
- _____

b. Interests
Write down what you like and dislike about the position.

Likes	Dislikes
_____	_____
_____	_____

c. Skills
Write down 5 skills that you would need to function in this position
- _____
- _____
- _____
- _____
- _____

d. Working environment
Write down 5 working conditions that are available in the company.

- _____
- _____
- _____
- _____
- _____

Figure 7.2.0 *Evaluating a job offer. Use the table above to evaluate your job offers.*

You can fill the assessment sheet above with the job profile that you created earlier in chapter 1. You can duplicate this sheet depending on how many offers you are trying to evaluate to have a clearer picture of the offer you should accept and the offer you should reject. It is also good for you to note that no job will completely match your desires, so you would have to think about your job priorities and determine the things that you can compromise and the ones that are not negotiable.

Try to let the interviewer know on time if you are declining a job offer. Sending a rejection letter late can make the recruiter feel like you have deliberately wasted their time. Letting the interview know on time that you would not be accepting the offer can save you the risk of burning your bridges at the early stages of your career.

Writing an acceptance or rejection letter

Whether you are accepting or rejecting a job offer, it is always good for you to put this in writing when you want to inform the interviewer about your decision. You don't expect the interviewer to assume or know that you have accepted the offer by keeping quite.

Even if you have not written an acceptance or rejection letter before, you can write one just following a few steps. These acceptance and rejection letter examples will help know how you can write your own.

Acceptance letter example

If you have been offered a job and you have decided to accept the offer, then it is good you do this formally. To accept a job offer formally, you can write an acceptance letter and send it to the recruiter. If you have never written an acceptance letter before, this example will guide you on writing one.
(Email Format)

Mr John.
ABC Group of Companies, Nigeria.
March 2nd, 2019.

Dear Mr John,
I just got a mail that I have been offered the position of a digital mar-keter in ABC Group of Companies and I am pleased to accept the offer. I really appreciate this opportunity. I am eager to make a positive contribution to the company and to also work with everyone in the

company.
I have also seen the salary break down for this position, and I am pleased with it. I look forward to resuming on April 1, 2020. If there is any additional information you require of me, please do let me know.
Once again, thank you very much for this opportunity.
(Signature)
(Name)

(Email letter)
Subject line: Janet Fieldstone - Job Offer Acceptance

Dear Mr.John,
I just got a mail that I have been offered the position of a digital marketer in ABC Group of Companies and I am pleased to accept the offer. I really appreciate this opportunity. I am eager to make a positive contribution to the company and to also work with everyone in the company.
I have also seen the salary break down for this position, and I am pleased with it.
I look forward to resuming on April 1, 2020. If there is any additional information you require of me, please do let me know.
Once again, thank you very much for this opportunity.
Regards.

Rejection letter example
Declining a job offer is not something that is easy to do. If you are sure that the job is not a good fit for you, then you go ahead and reject the offer.
It is good for you to spend time to go through the offer before you reject it, do you know why? Once you reject an offer there is hardly a chance that the employer will make you another offer. If you have considered the job offer and you have decided to decline, sending a polite and timely job offer rejection letter can help you maintain a good relationship with the employer.
So the question here is; how do you write a rejection letter and still sound polite. If you have never written a rejection letter

before, then this example will give you a heads up.

(Hard copy rejection letter)

Mr. John.
ABC Group of Companies, Nigeria.
March 2nd, 2019.

Dear Mr. John,
Thank you very much for offering me the position of a digital mar-
keter with ABC Group of Companies. It was not an easy decision to
make, but I have accepted a position with another company.
I honestly appreciate the time you spent during the interview and the
information you shared with me about the position and the com-
pany.
Thank you again for your consideration.
Sincerely,
(Signature)
Your name.

(Email rejection letter)
Dear Mr. John,
Thank you very much for offering me the position of a digital mar-
keter with ABC Group of Companies. It was not an easy decision to
make, but I have accepted a position with another company.
I honestly appreciate the time you spent during the interview and the
information you shared with me about the position and the com-
pany.

Thank you again for your consideration.
Regards.

7.3 NEGOTIATING THE JOB OFFER

When we talk about negotiating a job offer, most job seekers usually think about negotiating the salary. The salary is not the only thing that can be negotiated; you can negotiate other aspects of the offer based on what you want and what is important to you.

One fundamental thing you should note before you start negotiating your offer is research. You have to research the offer before and after the interview to know where to start your research from. It is important that you have useful information before you start negotiating the offer.

Since you know that researching the offer is important, the question here is; how do you research the offer?

Researching before the interview

It is best to start researching the company to find out basic information even before you go for the interview. Researching the salary ranges of the position that you are applying for will provide you with the appropriate salary information about the position and the company.

Research salary information of the company and the position on mysalaryscale.com, but don't end it there. Check for other employee reviews about the company to have an idea of the company culture and work environment. This research will give you an idea of what you should negotiate.

Researching during the interview

Always remember that the interview process is an opportunity for you to determine whether you are interested in the company or not. It is also good for you to take advantage of the interview to ask questions about things you would love to research on.

You can engage in a casual conversation with employees there to find out what parts of the offer can be negotiated. Finding out useful information from people in the company will definitely give you an idea of what you should negotiate.

Remember, throughout the interview process, your goal is to determine whether you are interested in working for this company and for this manager. It is up to you to ask questions during the process. It is always best to talk "off-the-record" with current or past employees to learn what items tend to get negotiated.

When you should start negotiating the offer

Technically, you should start negotiating when you have received an offer and have gotten the breakdown of the salary. Negotiating an offer before actually getting an offer can in most cases lead to your disqualification as a candidate.

An offer can be either verbal or written, also note that once an offer is made the salary details are revealed. Once you are made an offer, show enthusiasm for the job and ask how long it will take for you to evaluate the offer. You should put in mind that you are about to make a serious decision, you must arrange for a time to discuss the offer.

Negotiating your offer

Once you have fixed a date to discuss the offer, remember to show the employer that you are enthusiastic and happy about the job. If you don't seem happy about the job, then the employer will also be less interested in you.

Start negotiating your salary first, once you can win this aspect, you should be willing to step down or compromise your expectations regarding other aspects of the offer (benefits). Well, if you don't get the salary that you are targeting, you can push harder on other aspects of the offer.

Negotiation tips to keep in mind

- Don't make demands, ask questions instead.
- Make sure you are negotiating with authority.
- Be ready to let go.
- Make sure you are calm and be patient to wait for an answer.
- Make sure you don't focus on just your needs and wants, let the hiring manager see what is in it for them.
- Make sure you are in total control of your emotions.
- Be confident.
- Use the information you gathered during your research.
- Put it in writing. When you have decided to accept the offer, make sure you put it in writing for documentation purpose.

7.4 YOUR FIRST 90 DAYS ON THE JOB

Congratulations! All that you have worked for and dreamed of is finally here now, you have landed your dream job and you are to resume shortly. We can imagine how excited you are.

Landing a new job can send some form of anxiety down your spine, but at the same time; it is an exciting experience. It is exciting because you are embarking on a new journey, preparing to write your career journey on a clean slate.

Resuming at a new job can come with mixed feelings; first, you are excited about your new job, and then you are also anxious about the new job. This is because when you think about the new job, what comes to your mind is; new employer, new people, new environment, new systems, and practically new everyday right?

Considering all your thoughts and feelings about the new job, how do you position yourself for success within the first 90 days on the job? There is no formula for you to follow to achieve success within the first 90 days on your new job, but there are steps you can follow to achieve success. Always remember that the first 90 days on your new job is critical to your professional development within the company.

Since this is an important step to achieving career success, we have this guide to help you throughout the process.

Steps to take on your first day at work

This happens to be the most awkward day for most employees, but the following steps will make it much easy for you:

- Be prepared for anything: Keep an open and a welcoming mind, because anything can happen. The HR person can decide to take you on a tour around the office to show you around or someone might ask you to launch to start a conversation with you.
- Get to the office early. Get there even before the resumption time so that you can get relaxed quickly.
- Don't stay idle: if you have not been assigned with any task, ask the admin or any employee around if you can assist them with anything.

First 30 days on your new job

Acquaint Yourself with the Job and Environment
The first few days of your new job should be a time for you to acquaint yourself with your new job role and the work environment generally. The first rule to achieving success in a new workplace is to get comfortable around the new environment and people. Discomfort could lead to anxiety which is not healthy for you and your career at this stage.

To kill anxiety, you will need to take your time to gather all the information you need to succeed in working with these new set people and also undertaking a new task. Embrace every tool or assistance that you may be offered to perform your task.
Acquainting yourself with the new job will require you to create extra work time aside from the working hours to enable you to troubleshoot challenges that may likely occur while performing the task. Taking extra time to work with tools and aids will help you maximize your work time and will also increase your productivity during the first 90 days of your new job.

The following steps will help you acquaint yourself with your new job and environment;

- Be friendly, warm and open.

- Don't be shy to ask questions when you are not clear about something.
- Focus on the positive aspect of the new environment.

Be ready to Learn

One of the greatest ways you can achieve success during the first 90 days of your new job is opening yourself up to learning. Keep an open mind to learn from your colleagues. The truth about being in a new workplace is that even if you have to perform a role similar to what you have been doing in your previous place of employment there will still be something new for you to learn. If you are not learning a new role, then you are learning how it is done in the new company.

Opening yourself up to learning from everyone is a great path to achieving success during this period. If you actually want to achieve success during the first 90 days of your new job, then you have to be willing to learn and also willing to assist others with their task when the need arises. Helping others will also help to build your knowledge base over time combining the experiences you must have gathered.

Second 30 days on the new job (your second month)

Once you get past the first 30days, then here are the next sets of tips that can help you move past that as you begin to prepare for the next 60days.

Challenge Yourself and Add Value

Your goal should be channelled to how you can add value to the organization and make a positive difference in undertaking your task during the first 90 days of your new job. To achieve success within this period, you would need to challenge yourself to do more and add more value to the company.

Challenging yourself doesn't translate to being hard on yourself to take up extra tasks and overworking yourself beyond the limit. Challenging yourself simply means setting organizational goals within your capacity and making effort to achieve those goals over a period of time.

Setting goals that will challenge you to perform your task better will help you achieve success during the first few days of your new job.

Ask Questions

From research, we have noticed that the best and fastest way to learn is by being inquisitive. People that ask questions usually learn faster than those that don't ask any question at all. Developing an inquisitive mindset is a tool that can help you achieve maximum success during your first 90 days at work.

It is known that inquisitive people are great thinkers; they question and try to find out the reasons behind everything they are faced with. So developing the habit of asking questions can help you gain more understanding about the things you don't know or the things you struggle with.

Asking questions helps you cope better with the job and also facilitate your adaptation to the new situation. The following tips will help you ask well-timed questions;

- Think about what you want to know (you can put it in writing to make it more organized)
- Prioritize the information you need in order of importance
- Raise your questions at the appropriate time

Third 30 days on the job (your third month on the job)

By now you have spent about 60days. Now you should be preparing to get things revived up by doing the following:

Review your Work from Time to Time

One sure way to know if you are making progress or succeeding within the first 90 days in your new job is to review yourself from time to time. Evaluate your work every month to make sure you are still on track with the company's vision and goal. Taking a close evaluation of your role, and what you have been able to achieve within this period will help you discover areas that you need to pay more attention to, and maybe skills you may need to acquire to help you perform your task better.

In some organizations, a 90-day review for new employees is a common practice for performance evaluation. Even if your company doesn't have a formalized review, you can ask your supervisors or managers for an informal review. Asking your superiors to evaluate your performance will even help you know what they expect of you. Undertaking frequently review will help you achieve success fast within the first 90 days of work.

Keep Only Positive Perceptions

Achieving success actually starts from the mind. If you want to become successful within the first 90 days of your new job, then you should start planning to become successful in your mind first.

During the first 90 days of your new job, you may encounter some challenges trying to get used to the new role and environment. Even at this time, you should always focus on and develop positive perceptions only.

Welcoming only positive perceptions will help your relationship with your colleagues and also drive you towards achieving the goals you have set for yourself earlier during your first few weeks.

In many companies, during your first weeks, you may be undergoing training, so you would need to see every aspect of your learning process in the positive light.

You can keep a positive perception by;

- Creating an attitude of gratitude.
- Identifying a positive act as positive and not otherwise.

The first 90 days is one of the most important periods of your employment, and as such must be well prepared for. Achieving success during this period is mostly based on how much effort you put into the job.

7.5 FIRST 90 DAYS: BLUE PRINT TO SUCCEED AT YOUR NEW JOB

When you finally land a job, there are many things that come to your mind and many things that you probably have to deal with. Regardless of the many things that you have to deal with in your new job, one major thing you want to achieve in your new job is success.

This first 90 days blueprint will help you achieve success in the first 90 days of your new job.

30 Days	60 Days	90 Days
Establish Priorities	*Establish Priorities*	*Establish Priorities*
Priority 1	Priority 1	Priority 1
Priority 2	Priority 2	Priority 2
Priority 3	Priority 3	Priority 3
Set Goals	*Set Goals*	*Set Goals*
Goal 1	Goal 1	Goal 1
Goal 2	Goal 2	Goal 2
Goal 3	Goal 3	Goal 3
Land Marks	*Land Marks*	*Land Marks*
Land Mark 1	Land Mark 1	Land Mark 1
Land Mark 2	Land Mark 2	Land Mark 2
Land Mark 3	Land Mark 3	Land Mark 3
Outputs	*Outputs*	*Outputs*
- Analysis of the situation. - Recognition of priorities. - Plan for the next 30 days.	- Recognition of key resources. - Presentation of early assessment. - Plan for next 30 days.	Early achievements.
Manager's Review	*Manager's Review*	*Manager's Review*
- Situation conversation with manager. - Expectation conversation with manager. - Plan for the next 30 days.	Assess challenges and progress for the previous 30 days. Discuss next 30 days plan with manager.	Review results with manager

Figure 7.5.0 *First 90 days: Blue print to succeed. Use the table above to assess the first 90 days of your new job.*

If you go through the table above, you will notice that it guides you from the first 30 days to the last 30 days. Go through this table and succeed at your new job.

7.6 CHAPTER SUMMARY

Now, it is time for us to say a big congratulation to you, do you know why? It is because you have finally completed this book.

If you carefully read all the chapters and did all the assessments, then you are sure to succeed at whatever point you are at in your career. This book is designed to help through your job search journey from start to finish; it doesn't matter if you have never searched for a job before. This book will provide you with all you need to know to excel in your job search.

We are happy that you have all you need to excel at any stage of your job search journey. This book is designed to work you through all the stages of your job search journey; from examining yourself to preparing for job interviews to excelling at your first 90 days of your new job.

7.7 CONCLUSION

If you have successfully gone through all the sections of this book, then you have increased your chances of finding a job. If you have been applying for jobs over a period of time and have still not been able to land a job yet, it is normal for you to become disinterested in the job search process over time.

This book will give you a different experience regardless of how long you have been trying to get a job, this book is packed with tips, guides, and assessments that will help keep your job search on track. This book contains the entire guide you need to ensure you have a smooth job search journey from the first stage of discovering your career path, searching for opportunities, applying for jobs, preparing for interviews and right through your first days at work.

Always remember that as much as you are eager to get a job, employers are also eager to find the best candidate to fill their vacant position. Positioning yourself to be the "best job candidate" sure puts you ahead of other candidates.

Keep in mind that this book can be used at any time, so always remember to re-visit the book at every stage of your job search. This will ensure that you are on track and not forgetting anything.

RESOURCES

1. *Holland's codes of typology* (J.L. Holland (1997).
2. *Businessdictionary.com*
3. *Forbes Survey*
4. https://www.mcgill.ca/ caps
5. Jobvite survey

ABOUT THE BOOK

This book will provide you with current statistics, present job search context, and best practices for searching, applying for and getting jobs in the competitive job market. The awareness shared in this book will help you gain an understanding of the "world of work" with practical strategies for advancing your career.

ABOUT THE AUTHOR

Myjobmag

MyJobMag was founded and developed with the aim of making job search extremely easy for job seekers. At MyJobMag, our goal is to solve the fundamental employment challenge in Africa. From internship coaching, career counselling, training to personalized job discovery, we have got you covered. MyJobMag is not just a regular job listing platform but a career company leveraging technology to solve human resources and educational needs in Africa. Our mission is to efficiently connect great candidates to great companies at all levels while constantly developing both ends of the marketplace in diverse functional areas.